THE BRONZE AGE

Food Vessel from Argyllshire

THE BRONZE AGE

by

V. GORDON CHILDE, B.Litt.

F.R.A.I., F.S.A., F.S.A.Scot.

Professor of Prehistoric Archaeology
in the University of Edinburgh

BIBLO and TANNEN
New York
1963

First Published 1930
Reprinted by permission of
the Cambridge University Press

GN
777
.C5
1963

BIBLO and TANNEN
BOOKSELLERS and PUBLISHERS, Inc.
63 Fourth Avenue   New York 3, N.Y.

Library of Congress Catalog Card Number: 63-18050

Printed in U.S.A. by
NOBLE OFFSET PRINTERS, INC.
NEW YORK 3, N. Y.

CONTENTS

ILLUSTRATIONS

PREFACE

This book is intended to take up the story of prehistoric industrial development in North-western Europe from the point at which Mr M. C. Burkitt's *Our Early Ancestors* left it. While not a sequel to that work, mine presupposes such knowledge of general prehistory and the New Stone Age as may be found there and is intended to appeal to the same class of students. On the other hand, the nature and increased complexity of the material involves difference of treatment. And for the purposes of this more intensive study some of the divisions and classifications of the Bronze Age material, foreshadowed in one preliminary chapter of Mr Burkitt's book, have needed modification on lines explained here. Otherwise, I have refrained from duplicating his work save in so far as was necessary to make this book a complete and independent whole.

The bibliography aims primarily at indicating general works from which more detailed references can be obtained. Nevertheless some articles of outstanding importance or describing phases of Bronze Age civilization not yet adequately dealt with in larger comprehensive works have been included, even when they appear in comparatively obscure periodicals.

My thanks are due to the Society of Antiquaries of Scotland and to the Trustees of the British Museum for permission to reproduce figures; to Mrs M. C. Burkitt for her skilful re-drawing of some of the figures; and to Mr A. J. Edwards for reading the proofs.

V. GORDON CHILDE

EDINBURGH
1930

THE BRONZE AGE

CHAPTER I

THE IMPLICATIONS OF THE BRONZE AGE

THE story of human culture has long been divided conventionally into three main volumes according to the material generally employed for the principal cutting implements. At first our forerunners could only make knives and axes by chipping or grinding stone, bone or ivory. The period when such tools were alone in use is termed the Stone Age and constitutes the first volume. Mr Burkitt's books cited in the Bibliography give a good summary of its contents. The second volume opens when man has learned that certain kinds of stone may be compelled by heating under suitable conditions to yield a substance which, while hot, can be modelled or even run into a mould, but on cooling retains its shape and becomes harder and more durable than stone and takes as good an edge. This epoch is termed the Bronze Age—not very happily, since the first metal used industrially to any extent was copper; only by an accident in the areas where archaeology was first extensively studied—Denmark, England and France—was the copper already mixed with tin in the majority of early metal tools. The Bronze Age comes to an end when methods have been devised for extracting economically and working efficiently the much commoner metal, iron, which then replaces copper and its alloys in the manufacture of the crucial implements.

Thanks to the Epics, the Greeks were naturally well aware that the Iron Age in which they dwelt had been preceded by one in which "men used weapons of bronze

and wrought with bronze; for black iron was not".
But it is Lucretius who first expressly states that bronze
tools and weapons mark a stage intermediate between
the age of stone implements and the Iron Age he knew.
A Dane, Thomsen, revived or rediscovered Lucretius'
division early last century. And the tripartite division
was soon applied also to England, France, Germany
and Italy.

In these regions the system works admirably. A well-
defined group of remains from tombs and villages can
be assigned to a period of time when bronze was current
but anterior to the adoption of iron. Yet in this sense
the Bronze Age occupies a disproportionately short
epoch in our series. The Stone Age had lasted a hundred
thousand years or so; the Iron Age in Great Britain is
already two thousand five hundred years old and seems
as vigorous as ever. Against this the Bronze Age in
Britain can only claim fifteen hundred or, on the most
generous estimate, two thousand years. But, if in Northern Europe bronze played a leading rôle in industry
for a relatively short span of years, in the Aegean area,
Egypt, Mesopotamia and the Indus valley, bronze, or
at least copper, had been in regular use for fully twice
as long. And those three or four thousand years witnessed man's first emergence from barbarism to civilization, the foundation of the first cities, the harnessing of
animal motive power, the invention of writing, the
establishment of consciously ordered government, the
beginnings of science, the specialization and consequent
perfection of the primary industrial arts, and the inaugu-
ration of international trade and intercourse. Hence our
Bronze Age volume makes up in wealth of incident for
its modest bulk.

All the vital elements of modern material culture are

immediately rooted in the Bronze Age though their presuppositions may go back to the closing phase of the Stone Age (the so-called Neolithic Period). Nay more; modern science and industry not only go back to the period when bronze was the dominant industrial metal, their beginnings were in a very real sense conditioned and inspired by the mere fact of the general employment of bronze or copper. It is worth while considering briefly the presuppositions of such a general use of metal in order to make the point plain.

In the first place it implies a knowledge of the radical transformation of the physical properties of the substance by heat. The first smiths had discovered that a hard and intractable reddish substance, copper, became malleable and plastic on heating. You may even pour it like water into a vessel, but on cooling it becomes as hard as ever, assuming now the shape of the receptacle. Of course metallic copper occurs "native" in nature. By hammering, it may be shaped into imitations of the simpler forms of stone or bone tools. The Indians of Ohio employed the native metal in this way and treated it as a peculiarly workable sort of stone, hammering it without the aid of heat. But such an application of Stone Age processes to native copper does not mark the beginnings of the age of metals. There is no reason to suppose that it led directly thereto. The superiority of copper over stone or horn lies in its being fusible and malleable. It can be shaped by casting into forms the old materials could never assume, and the material in itself imposes no limit to the size of the object to be fashioned from it. A piece of stone or bone can only be shaped by chipping, grinding or cutting bits *off* it; your molten copper is completely plastic: you may use as little or as much as you want without impairing its solidity; you may even weld pieces together indissolubly by heating and hammering.

The change in the properties of copper by heat is really very startling; it is distinctly more dramatic than the effect of baking upon potter's clay. By that process a vessel is certainly rendered durable and deprived of porosity. But the form and the texture are not superficially altered. Moreover the process is irreversible. It is a far greater leap from solid cold copper to the glowing liquid metal, yet the change can be produced as often as desired. To recognize the continuity underlying such transformations, to appreciate their practical significance and to devise means for their control demanded a power of inference and synthesis unusual in barbarians. The discoverers must implicitly make the distinction between substance and its appearances and so may justly claim a place among the founders of science.

The effective utilization of the discoveries just analysed involved the elaboration of a highly complicated technique through a series of inventions. The masters of these mysteries, the first smiths, were perhaps the first independent craftsmen. Any hunter or farmer could make a flint knife or arrow-head and grind out a stone axe-head in his spare time. His wife could stitch together robes of skins, even spin and weave, and mould and fire clay pots. The art of the smith was so complicated that prolonged apprenticeship was required. His labour was so long and exacting that it could not be performed just in odd moments of leisure; it was essentially a full-time job. And the smith's products were so important to the community that those engaged directly in food production must provide for his primary needs in addition to their own. Among primitive peoples to-day the smith always does enjoy just such a privileged position as might be expected. In a Bronze Age village we often find one hut, but never more, that was obviously the smithy. In a Neolithic village on the contrary no certain traces of industrial specialization are often detectable.

Even more startling and mysterious were the trans-mutations involved in the extraction of the metal. As we have noted, metallic copper occurs in nature, but with a few exceptions, notably in North America and South Africa, only in minimal quantities. In all other regions, before copper could come into general use, the metal must be extracted from its ores—oxides, sulphides, silicates or carbonates—by a chemical process termed reduction. Copper ores are crystalline or amorphous substances, greenish blue, red or grey in colour, found in veins in old metamorphic or eruptive rocks. What could be more startling than the evocation from these greenish or grey stones, crystalline or powdery in tex-ture, of the tough malleable red metal! Here is a complete transmutation of the very nature of a material! The process of reduction is indeed simple enough; heat in contact with charcoal will effect it. But it was a stupendous feat of generalization on the part of the barbarian to connect green crystalline stones with the tough red metal. The recognition of the underlying continuity marked the beginning of chemistry.

The discovery of silver, lead and tin would be a natural corollary. The possessors of these secrets would easily gain credit for supernatural powers among bar-barians to whom all stones looked much alike. They would constitute a class or guild no less powerful than the smiths. It would be their task to search out and smelt the peculiar stones that would yield the coveted metals.

Copper ores in small quantities and of poor quality are very widely distributed. No doubt early man often exploited lodes that are so poor or have been so thoroughly worked in the past that they are no longer mentioned in text-books on mining geology. And surface lodes were certainly once plentiful. But the time would soon come when such deposits had been exhausted and the prospectors must burrow underground for their ore. Mining for flint had been practised in the Stone Age, but it was a comparatively simple matter to dig pits and cut galleries in the chalk (where the good flints occur). Metal ores are embedded in very hard rock that can only be cut with difficulty to-day. The exploitation of copper on a large scale implied the solution of delicate problems in mining engineering[19]. The Bronze Age miners of Europe knew how to split rock by kindling fire against it and then throwing water on it; they had worked out methods of timbering subterranean galleries and had devised pulley-buckets for raising the ore. A curious sidelight on the unity of early metallurgy is provided by the discovery in all ancient mines that have been examined, whether in the Caucasus, Sinai, Austria, Spain or Britain, of grooved hammer-stones (i.e. stones girt with an artificial groove to receive the binding thongs with which they were hafted at the end of a split stick).

A further chemical discovery was involved in the advanced metallurgy of the Bronze Age. The addition to copper of a small proportion of tin reduces its melting-point, minimizes the danger of flaws from bubbles in casting and increases the hardness of the cold alloy. Here was another transmutation, the combination of two dissimilar substances to produce a third different from both. The alloy can be obtained either by smelting together the ores of tin and copper, or by melting tin (or tin ore) with copper. In the first instance the alloy may have been produced accidentally through the use of a copper ore with which tin was mixed. It is, for instance, curious that in Mesopotamia tin-bronze was comparatively common before 3000 B.C. but becomes rare after that date(11). A possible explanation is that the Sumerians had unconsciously been using a stanniferous ore the supplies of which gave out or were cut off by 3000. In any case it seems certain that by then they were deliberately trying to produce the superior metal and seeking substitutes, adding, for instance, lead. What is still more significant, by 2000 B.C. the mixture now universally admitted to give the best results, of one part tin to nine of copper, had already been recognized as the standard combination. That implies a great deal of critical examination—i.e. experiment in the modern sense—since there is nothing in nature to suggest those particular proportions.

Experiments were also made with other alloys. In Hungary, the Baltic lands, and the Caucasus antimony was sometimes used as a substitute for tin. We have mentioned the possibility of a similar use of lead by the Sumerians. Brass, an alloy of copper and zinc, has on the other hand not been found before the Iron Age.

Thirdly, in addition to the physical and chemical discoveries just described, the general use of metal presupposes regular and extensive trade relations. It is indeed true that copper ores are fairly widely distributed and that in early days poor lodes, now exhausted or at least uneconomical, were exploited. None the less the sources are definitely limited. The supplies are situated almost exclusively in mountainous regions; the great civilizations of the Orient grew up in river valleys entirely lacking in any ores. Similarly the most populous centres of Neolithic culture in Europe, the löss lands of Central Europe, the Ukraine, and Denmark, are some way from the nearest copper lodes. Regular communications must be established between Egypt and Sinai, between Sumer and the Zagros or Caucasus, between Denmark and the Eastern Alps, Slovakia or England, before even copper could be regularly used there.

The position is still worse when bronze and not pure[1] copper is demanded; for now two foreign products are needed one of which is distinctly rare. Tin occurs certainly in the Malay Peninsula, South Africa, Khorasan, Tuscany, the Bohemian Erzgebirge, Western and Southern Spain, Southern France, Brittany and Cornwall, probably also in the Caucasus and Syria and possibly even in Central Greece. Only in the Caucasus, Bohemia, Spain and Cornwall do copper lodes occur in any proximity to the tin ores. In most cases, therefore, the use of bronze would involve trade in two distinct metals that must be brought to a single meeting-point from different quarters. The extant evidence suggests, for instance, that Central European and Scandinavian bronze-workers drew their copper from Slovakia or the Austrian Alps and their tin from Bohemia or sometimes England.

At the same time, within a given ethnic group the individual farmer must sacrifice his economic inde-

[1] Chemically pure copper could not have been prepared by the ancients and would have had no special value for them. In this book "pure" means "without intentional alloy". The accidental impurities found in all ancient copper are valuable as indicating the source of the ore used in the several regions. For instance, the high nickel content of early Sumerian and Indus copper suggests that both civilizations were drawing on the ores from Oman which show a high nickel content.

pendence and the village its self-sufficiency as the price of the new material. Each Neolithic household could manufacture the requisite knives, axe-heads and awls of flint, stone or bone; the Neolithic village need never look beyond its own domains for the necessary material —nor did, save in the case of luxury articles such as shells. But metal tools the farmer must, as we have already seen, purchase from the expert, the village smith. And the latter must, except in exceptional circumstances, import his raw materials from outside the communal boundaries. This is perhaps the essential difference between the Neolithic and Bronze Ages. The most striking feature of a Neolithic community was its self-sufficiency. The sacrifice of that self-sufficiency was only possible when certain sociological and economic conditions had been fulfilled and brought in its train a series of other political and industrial changes. That in itself would explain why the Bronze Age did not begin simultaneously all over the world or even all over Europe. Peoples develop at unequal rates, and the effective demand for and use of metal is only possible when a certain stage of development has been reached.

The development of internal and foreign commerce implied in a Bronze Age presupposes a certain degree of political stability. One of the economic foundations of the first Egyptian State was the exploitation of the copper lodes of Sinai as a State enterprise by periodical expeditions supported by the royal armies. Similarly trade must go hand in hand with improvement in the means of communication. The wheeled car and the sailing ship appear in the Ancient East as heralds of the age of metals. The same commercial needs must at least have given an impulse to the development of writing and seal-cutting. Letters and contracts dealing with trade bulk largely in any collection of Babylonian documents. And seals served in place of a signature (for few could master the ancient scripts) as well as to put a *tabu* upon the object sealed.

The general propositions just enunciated involve some archaeological corollaries specially germane to the subject of this book. The discoveries and inventions implicit in metal-working are so abstruse and complex that independent origin at several points—in the Old World at any rate—is excluded as fantastically improbable; knowledge of the essential techniques must, that is to say, have been diffused from some centre. The uniformity of processes throughout the Ancient East and Europe at the dawn of the Bronze Age affords some positive justification for the diffusionist assumption[7]. It is, indeed, quite likely that miners and smiths constituted distinct crafts or even castes, membership of which implied initiation but conferred some degree of immunity from the bondage of tribal custom. We must then envisage the spread of the knowledge of metal as a dual process: on the one hand we should expect a distribution of metal objects by trade comparable to the spread of European firearms among contemporary savages. The diffusion of metallurgical knowledge, on the other hand, must be associated with an actual spread of initiates either as prospectors voyaging in quest of ore, or as perambulating smiths seeking their fortunes by plying their trade among barbarians, or as slaves or others who have secured initiation in the original centre or one of its offshoots, returning home. These two processes must be kept distinct. The first may produce a chalcolithic age in a given region; i.e. a few metal objects may be imported and used side by side with native tools of stone and imitated locally in flint or bone.

A true Bronze Age can only arise with the advent of metallurgists or smiths.

Even so, the substitution of metal for stone tools and weapons must inevitably be a gradual process. It will take a long period of education and considerable commercial organization before the peasant farmer finds it cheaper to buy, say a bronze sickle, than to make one at home out of flint. A long interval will accordingly elapse after the introduction of bronze before it has finally ousted stone. So in Egypt agricultural implements continued to be made out of flint down to the New Kingdom or for nearly two thousand years after metal had become reasonably common. In Bronze Age settlements and graves in Europe too even well-made stone axe-heads (celts) occur. Not all stone tools therefore are Neolithic, nor is their presence incompatible with a Bronze Age date.

We must equally beware of attaching too great importance to the use of pure copper. A regular supply of tin involves, as we have seen, more extensive commercial relations than the corresponding supply of copper. The advantages of bronze would not in all circumstances counterbalance its much higher price. During the third millennium pure copper was largely used in Mesopotamia though bronze was known even before 3000 B.C., in Egypt only copper was employed, and in the Aegean bronze was rare and generally poor in tin (i.e. with less than the standard 10 per cent.). In continental Europe a large number of tools and weapons of pure copper may be assigned to a period anterior to the local Bronze Age on account of their form and context. This period may be justly styled a "Copper Age" or "the Copper Age" with some qualification, such as "in Hungary". At the same time, there are other objects of pure copper or very poor bronze that none the less belong to an advanced phase of the local Bronze Age. The negative result of analysis in this case does not indicate high antiquity but merely an interruption of the tin supply in the region where the objects were cast— an historical event explicable in economic or political terms.

Again it is obvious that the regular use of metal would not begin simultaneously everywhere. The mystery can only be imparted to those in contact with its masters. It will radiate slowly from the centre. It will reach only those who have something to offer the smith or the prospector; these can utilize their knowledge only in so far as they control supplies of ore or can obtain the requisite raw material by trade or political action. Actually metallurgy was being practised in Mesopotamia and Egypt during the fourth millennium B.C., at the beginning of the third it had been implanted in the Aegean area whence it was diffused up the Danube valley and along the Mediterranean and Atlantic coasts. The Bronze Age in Bohemia and Britain begins about 2000 B.C., in Denmark about 1600, in Siberia perhaps six centuries later. In the Pacific islands it never began at all.

The earlier stages of this process in which the actual discovery of metallurgy took place lie outside the scope of this book, which is devoted primarily to the Bronze Age of North-western and Central Europe. Nothing comparable to the extraordinary civilizations that had grown up by 3000 B.C. in the valleys of the Nile, the Tigris-Euphrates and the Indus existed north of the Alps till Caesar came with his legionaries. No description of the Oriental cultures and no sketch of their rise could usefully be compressed within the compass of these pages. But we ask our readers to remember, when picturing the lives of their barbarian ancestors who reared round barrows on the Downs and lived in hut-circles on the moors, that the Royal Tombs of Ur had long been forgotten, and the Pyramids were already hoary with age. The great temples of Karnak and the palaces of Knossos are roughly contemporary with our stone circles, and few, if any, of our hill forts can compare in age even with the acropolis of Mycenae. But though a worthy description is impracticable here, the Oriental and East Mediterranean civilizations exercised such a profound influence on Bronze Age Europe, inspiring and moulding her metallurgical traditions, that their authors must be at least named if the sequel is to be intelligible. Moreover, the chronology of illiterate Europe rests entirely upon archaeological synchronisms with cultural phases dated by the written records of Egypt and Sumer.

On the banks of the Nile in Upper Egypt[9] a series of graves, arrangeable by typological[1] study in a regular sequence, reveals the progress in industries and arts of peasant communities down to the time, about 3400–3100 B.C., when a king of Upper Egypt, traditionally known as Menes, united the whole land under a single sceptre. The record begins at a remote period, termed the Badarian (after a site near Assiout[8]) when enough rain still fell in Upper Egypt for big trees to grow where now all is sand. That implies a climatic regime approximating to that ruling in North Africa during the European Ice Age, when the great belt of heavy cold air (termed an arctic anticyclone) over our glaciers diverted southward the rain-bearing Atlantic squalls (cyclones). We are therefore at latest in what in Europe

[1] Typology as used here is defined on p. 53 below.

would be the Mesolithic Age. But the Badarian villagers on the Nile were already farmers enjoying a culture comparable to that of the fellahin to-day: they could make beautiful pots, grind vases out of hard stone, weave linen, plait baskets, flake flint superbly, put a glaze on stone beads and carve ivory into combs, pins and figurines. They were also able to obtain shells from the Red Sea and malachite, probably from Sinai, by some sort of trade. They were even acquainted with metallic copper since beads and a pin of the metal have been found in their graves. The Badarians had been accustomed to paint their eyes with malachite, a carbonate of copper. The metal might have been discovered by the reduction of a little of this paint dropped on to the glowing ashes of a hearth. Still it would not be correct to say that the Badarians were metallurgists or lived in a copper age.

The same remark is true of the succeeding period, termed Early Predynastic or Amratian. The communities are now bigger, trade relations have been extended so that even lapis lazuli from Afghanistan, obsidian from Armenia or Melos, coniferous woods from Syria and gold from Nubia were available. Even copper objects are more numerous than before, but all are of perfectly simple forms that might easily have been obtained by cold working in imitation of bone and flint models.

Genuinely metallic types that presuppose a knowledge of casting are first found late in the third phase, termed Middle Predynastic or Gerzean. But now changes in pottery, dress and weapons denote the cultural subjugation of Upper Egypt to a new power, immediately centred in the unexplored Delta but very possibly Asiatic in origin. The metal objects of the period, that are indeed very sparse, may be products of a school of metallurgy created by the (unknown) Early Predynastic inhabitants of Lower Egypt or directly inspired by some external centre in Asia. Some elements in Middle Predynastic culture certainly came from the latter quarter. In any case the clash of native African and Asiatic traditions caused a general spurt in culture, mirrored in progress and specialization in all the arts. At the same time accumulation of wealth and its concentration in individual hands are marked by the elaboration of some tombs and an increasing range in the comparative wealth of the grave goods.

In the Late Predynastic or Semainian phase the dual traditions traceable in Middle Predynastic times were fused. Moreover continued accumulation of wealth in a country, bereft of ore, building stone and timber, rendered necessary and possible an extension and regularization of trade, till Egypt was at last in contact with another civilization that had grown up in the Tigris-Euphrates valley. Concomitantly industry was further specialized to the great benefit of most crafts, though the pots of this period, being regular factory products, are far less attractive than the more individual creations of earlier times. Some favourably situated villages grew into real towns, and the chief of one of them, Abydos, that commanded one main caravan route to the Red Sea and the East, was eventually able to master the whole land to the Mediterranean coasts, founding what is termed the First Dynasty (about 3100 B.C.).

From this point the written record supplements the archaeological. We see the royal arms extended to the copper mines of Sinai and then the colonization of Byblos in North Syria to secure control of the cedars of

Lebanon. Therewith we arrive at the Old Kingdom, Dynasties III to VI, which witnessed the building of the Pyramids, but eventually collapsed into anarchy through internal exhaustion and Asiatic aggression.

The country rose again under the Middle Kingdom, Dynasties XI–XIII (2000–1780 B.C.), only to collapse once more beneath the onslaught of the barbarian invaders known as the Hyksôs.

The greatest period in Egyptian history followed the national revolt against the invaders led by the Seventeenth Dynasty and completed under the Eighteenth (beginning 1580 B.C.). The Thothmes reconquer Syria and Palestine; the Amenhoteps conduct diplomacy in quite modern style with the kings of Babylonia, Assyria and the Cappadocian Hittites. In alliance with the latter the Rameses repel the assaults of the Philistines and the Sea-Peoples from the North, some of whom at least were Europeans. But eventually these barbarians wrecked the Empire and incidentally ended the Bronze Age in the Near East.

No such clear record is yet available of the rise of civilization in Mesopotamia. The ancient records name kings reigning for fabulous years before what the Sumerians termed the Flood. Remains of the prediluvian civilization have in fact recently come to light at Ur and al'Ubaid in Sumer and at Kish farther north, covered thickly by the clay left by a huge inundation(11). They disclose already highly civilized communities living in towns or at least large villages. The splendid painted pottery from these levels connects the oldest culture of the Mesopotamian plain with a great province covering the whole Iranian plateau and extending eastward perhaps to the Indus. Its best known representative is the "first city" at Susa in Elam(10). The prediluvian culture(8), of unknown antiquity and antecedents, boasted all the arts of Early Predynastic Egypt with the addition of mature metallurgy. Copper was not only known at Susa I, it was freely used for axe-heads and even mirrors fashioned by casting.

In Mesopotamia, upon the eight feet of sterile clay left by the Flood above the prediluvian houses, stand the foundations of the oldest historical cities, built by a literate people known to us as Sumerians. These folk, distinguished by language and dress, lived in City States, normally autonomous but each striving for, and sometimes securing, the mastery over all the rest. Palaces and graves recently uncovered at Kish reveal the advanced civilization ruling under the first dynasty to attain to hegemony after the Flood. Even more startling are the Royal Tombs recently explored at Ur and perhaps in some cases even older than the historical First Dynasty of Ur, dated round about 3100 B.C. By that date, in any case, the Sumerians enjoyed a settled polity and had attained a level of industrial skill far ahead of First Dynasty Egypt. In particular they used metals to an extent and with a skill never dreamed of on the Nile till New Kingdom times. Egypt possessed abundant supplies of good flint, and that material was used there exclusively in agriculture and very generally by the poorer classes as a whole till quite late. The alluvial plain of Mesopotamia had nothing similar to offer its occupants and so, the raw material for cutting tools having to be imported in any case, the durable copper really came cheaper than flint. That implied a dependence on foreign trade even greater than Egypt's. The variety of exotic substances found in Sumerian graves and above all the discovery of seals, actually manufactured in distant India, illustrate the success with which that need was met. Conversely, while most distinctive Egyptian metal types are peculiar to the Nile valley, Sumerian forms lie at the base of South Russian and Central European metallurgy.

The early Sumerian period, thus inaugurated, is often termed pre-Sargonic; for a well-defined era ends when a Semitic prince, whose name has been simplified to Sargon, made his city, Akkad or Agadé, supreme throughout Mesopotamia. He is said even to have reached the Mediterranean. After the collapse of his empire, civilization largely stagnated in Iraq; in particular no fresh metal types were created. Historically a new era is marked by the rise of Babylon to the hegemony under Hammurabi's dynasty (First Dynasty of Babylon, *circa* 2100 B.C.). Thereafter Babylon remained the political capital of an united Babylonia for close on fifteen hundred years.

West of the "prediluvian" cultural domain began a province, centred in Anatolia and once perhaps embracing Crete, characterized by dark-faced carboniferous pots imitating gourd vessels. Round about 3000 B.C. the secrets of metallurgy began to reach this area rich in ores, probably from Mesopotamia. About the same time the local potter commenced producing a red ware by baking his pots over a clear fire in an oxidizing atmosphere. One branch of this culture then occupied Cyprus(18), attracted no doubt by the metal wealth of the island that has given its name to copper. Another branch pushed into Thrace and Macedonia. The most interesting, however, developed a higher civilization on the hill of Hissarlik(3), a point on the Dardanelles that commanded at once the sea ways from the Aegean to the Black Sea, the Danube and the Caucasus and the terminus of the land route from Mesopotamia across

Asia Minor with its transmarine extensions into Thrace,
Macedonia and Central Europe. Out of a large village
(known as Troy I) at this strategic point there arose
during the third millennium an important town termed
Troy II on whose ruins the Homeric Troy (Troy VI)
was later to rise.

The citadel of Troy II was girt with a strong wall of
stone surmounted by brick battlements. Within stood
palatial buildings of the so-called megaron[1] type. The
citadel and its encircling walls were rebuilt twice so that
three structural phases are recognizable. The last of
these probably belongs already to Middle Aegean times
(see p. 21). Shortly after 2000 B.C. the city was razed
to the ground, but its defenders had found time to bury
many of their treasures. The latter escaped the eyes of
the invaders and were first rediscovered by H. Schliemann between A.D. 1873 and 1879. Our knowledge of
Trojan metallurgy is almost entirely derived from these
hoards(17) which should belong to what is called the
Middle Aegean Period. After the sack the site was occupied only by minor villages till, towards the middle of
the sixteenth century B.C., a new and larger city arose, the
Homeric Troy that the Achaeans sacked about 1200 B.C.

Metal-using civilization impinged upon Crete and
the Aegean islands from two quarters, Anatolia-Syria
and Egypt. Crete(12) had already been occupied in
Neolithic times by people of Anatolian affinities. The
metal-using civilization termed Minoan begins rather
before 3000 B.C. with the advent of Nilotic immigrants,
possibly refugees flying from Menes when he conquered
the Delta. At the same time powerful influences and
very possibly immigrants from the East reached the

---

[1] A "megaron" is essentially a long hall with a central hearth,
preceded by a pillared porch on the short side.

island, and Cretan metallurgy is largely based upon Asiatic traditions. The life of the Minoan civilization is divided into three main periods, Early, Middle and Late Minoan (abbreviated E.M., M.M. and L.M. respectively) each in turn subdivided into three phases distinguished by the Roman numerals I, II, or III.

Already in Early Minoan times Crete enjoyed a genuine urban civilization. The people lived largely by maritime trade, even building their towns on barren islets or headlands, quite unsuited to farmers but affording excellent harbours.

During the same period the stoney little islands of the Aegean (Cyclades), that had offered no sustenance to Neolithic peasants[10] but were rich in copper, emery, marble, or obsidian, and afforded convenient halting-places on voyages across the Aegean, were occupied by prospectors from Anatolia. On them grew up a flourishing maritime culture termed Early Cycladic[16]. Its monuments, strongholds girt with walls of stone and graves of varied form, suggest a less refined and less pacific civilization than the Minoan, but one in which metallurgy flourished and where distinctive metal types were created. The islanders were in regular commercial contact with Crete, Troy and mainland Greece.

In the latter area an older layer of Neolithic peasants was overlaid by groups of more industrial and mercantile immigrants, allied to the islanders and to the Macedonian wing of the Anatolians. These new-comers occupied principally seaports and sites on land trade routes[14] extending as far west as Levkas[15]. Their culture is known as Early Helladic and in respect of metallurgy was mainly dependent upon Troy and the Cyclades, though the use of a glazed paint was probably derived from Crete.

The Minoan, Cycladic and Helladic cultures, sharing in a common trade, were all in constant intercommunication. Hence it is possible to correlate the several stages of culture in each area and to extend the Minoan system to the whole Aegean world. Crete in particular, being in regular touch with Egypt, the phases of Aegean culture may be approximately dated in terms of solar years. The period just surveyed, termed Early Aegean, extends from about 3100 to 2100 B.C. On the islands and in mainland Greece the beginning of the Middle Aegean period is not very well defined, since no radical changes took place before Middle Aegean II times(13).

The Middle Minoan period in Crete, on the contrary, witnessed the concentration of power and wealth in the hands of princes ruling in the centre of the island commanding the great road that linked the sea-routes from Egypt with those to Greece and the Black Sea. By M.M. II, Knossos, near the northern terminal of the road, was the undisputed capital of the island. Here rose frescoed palaces, often destroyed by seismic or political cataclysms, but continually resuscitated down to L.M. III. Sir Arthur Evans has rediscovered Homer's broad Knossos, the seat of Minos, and the "dancing-ground" laid out by Daedalus. And frescoes on the palace walls depict the ritual games of bull-grappling that inspired the legend of the Minotaur.

Towards M.M. II times Crete had so far monopolized Aegean trade that the Cyclades' prosperity declined and many islands were deserted. At the same time, Middle Helladic II[1], a new folk, conveniently, if

[1] Numbering the phase according to the contemporary Cretan periods. Messrs Wace and Blegen, owing to the absence of any sharp break at a point contemporary with the Cretan M.M. I, prefer to term this phase M.H. I, while admitting its contemporaneity with M.M. II.

incorrectly, termed Minyans, gained the upper hand on the Greek mainland and adjacent islands from Aegina to Levkas. They were more martial and less industrial than their Early Helladic predecessors, but far from barbarians.

Then towards 1600 B.C. a Minoan prince gained a footing at Mycenae on the Peloponnese. His remains and those of his family were found by H. Schliemann in the famous Shaft Graves, dug on the slope of the acropolis and included within the city walls. Sir Arthur Evans has, however, adduced convincing grounds for believing that the prince's body had originally reposed in the great beehive tomb, built into the hillside outside the walls and known since the days of Pausanias as the Treasury of Atreus, a tomb that Mr Wace dates some three centuries later (L.H. III) and attributes to the last monarch of a different dynasty.

In L.M. I and II Crete attained the zenith of her power, the most grandiose phase of the palace of Knossos belonging to L.M. II. During the same period the Minoan civilization was extended to the mainland. A whole series of stately beehive tombs along the western coasts and at the head of gulfs facing south as far as Volo in Thessaly and palaces adorned with frescoes in Minoan style mark the seats of the Cretan dynasts.

This imperialist expansion overtaxed the island's strength. At the beginning of L.M. III Knossos and the other palaces were sacked and not rebuilt, though the towns continued to flourish. The mainland, however, progressed. Mycenae was now the capital of the Aegean world as in Homer's lays. She was girt with a megalithic wall of "Cyclopean" masonry as were Tiryns, Athens and other citadels within which rose palaces of the megaron plan, very different architecturally from the

Cretan, though decked with frescoes of Minoan technique. A provincial variant of the Minoan culture,
termed Late Mycenaean, ruled all over the mainland
and extended to many of the islands and even Cyprus.
Trade was more extensive than ever, and even Mycenaean vases were exported to Anatolia, Syria, Palestine,
Egypt and Sicily. But about 1250 B.C., when the
Egyptian records are already preoccupied with "unrest
among the Isles of the Sea", these peaceful relations
were broken off. The Mycenaean culture in a decadent
form, L.M. III *b*, however, persisted for a couple of
centuries and even spread to Macedonia. During this
period we find northern types of sword and other
indications of influences from beyond the Balkans. In
Macedonia even a barbaric pottery, apparently of
Hungarian antecedents, intrudes in and above the last
ruins of the plundered Mycenaean settlements.

The Iron Age in the Aegean begins about this point
without any complete break with late Mycenaean traditions, at least in Southern Greece and Crete. The metal
that now replaced bronze in the manufacture of cutting
implements had been used occasionally for that purpose
even in the fourteenth century. The Hittite records
show that it was then being manufactured in Kizwadana,
an unidentified locality under the control of the Cappadocian Hittites. By L.M. III *b* times there are traces
of iron-working in Macedonia, and soon after 1200 B.C.
it was generally practised in Asia Minor and then in
Crete and Greece.

Having now surveyed the civilized world of the
Ancient East, we can conclude this chapter with a
glance at the question, "Where did the revolutionary
discovery of metallurgy originate?" It is, of course,
theoretically possible that the properties of copper were

independently realized in Egypt and Hither Asia, or even in illiterate Spain and Hungary, and that the barbarians of Cornwall and Bohemia spontaneously hit upon the alloy, known before 3000 b.c. in Sumer and India. Practically, in the case of the Old World where the first metal-using civilizations had such wide foreign relations and were bound together by so many common traits, no one, unprejudiced by the passions evoked by a perverse diffusionism, will suggest that all the complex processes involved were elaborated separately at two or more comparatively adjacent points in Eurasia. Really the question resolves itself into one of the comparative claims of Egypt and the Asiatic cultural province designated "prediluvian".

It must be admitted and indeed insisted that by 3000 b.c. Egyptian and Sumerian metallurgy constituted two distinct schools. Any competent archaeologist could distinguish, as our Chapter III will show, between a proto-dynastic Egyptian celt, dagger or spear-head and an equally early Sumerian specimen, to say nothing of more specialized types such as pins or earrings. But as we go back, the differences tend to vanish.

In the Nile valley the conditions for the rise of metallurgy were admittedly fulfilled, even though no supplies of ore were available locally(21). The copper objects from Badarian and Early Predynastic graves, the oldest samples of metal to which any sort of date can be assigned, strongly suggest that the copper ore used as eye-paint was in fact there reduced to the metallic state and the product utilized. Yet nothing from these periods proves that the process was applied deliberately or systematically, still less that the properties of metal were realized or employed(10). Only in Middle Predynastic times do we meet implements of any size or of

a distinctively metallic character—the results of casting
in a mould. And even these are rare and sporadic.
Moreover, in the Middle Predynastic culture we encounter types, foreign to the earlier periods but common
at all times in Hither Asia. I may instance the pear-
shaped stone mace-head that replaces the Early Predynastic disk-shaped type, spouted vases and dark-on-
light vase-painting. Even under the early dynasties,
when metallurgy was fully understood and quite individual types were created, flint remained in common use
for reasons already explained.

Now Egypt is exceptionally favoured from the ex-
cavator's point of view. It has long enjoyed a civilized
government; a delightful winter climate makes it the
resort of the wealthy of all Europe. The mighty stone
monuments that geographical circumstances enabled
the ancient Egyptians to erect and that climatic conditions have conspired to preserve, have inspired the
less stupid of such visitors to serious excavations as a
diversion and encouraged the rest to subsidize profes-
sional diggers. Mesopotamia, on the other hand, remote,
inhospitable winter and summer, and long misruled by
a corrupt Old Turkey, has only been seriously explored
during the last ten years. Persia, even more inaccessible
and climatically forbidding, is closed to excavation by a
monopoly granted to an incompetent and bankrupt
nation. And in India the British Government was content to allow the ruins of ancient cities to be used as
ballast for railway lines. Under these circumstances it
is difficult to compare the prediluvian culture with the
predynastic or to gauge its origin, extent and antiquity.
Still its highland home is rich in metals including even
tin. And as far back as we can trace the culture, it was
associated with genuinely metallic and often highly

developed copper implements. Descending to the alluvial plain, its authors would find copper cheaper to import than flint.

Early Sumerian metallurgy, which seems descended directly from the prediluvian, was certainly superior to the contemporary Egyptian both in extent and in the quality of its products. For example, in Sumer bronze was known and core-casting regularly employed. The marked superiority of Sumerian metallurgy over the Egyptian, at the first moment when contemporary objects from the two countries can be compared, affords some presumption in favour of the higher antiquity of the Asiatic industry. The metal work of Middle Predynastic Egypt would in that case be inspired from Asia. The force of this argument is, however, somewhat diminished by persistent uncertainties as to the precise dates of the First Dynasties in Egypt and Ur respectively and by the fact that after the Second Dynasty Egyptian civilization was on the whole, though not in metallurgy, ahead of Sumerian. The latter objection is to some extent discounted when we recall that the political unification of Egypt placed the labour power of the whole population at the disposal of Pharaoh for the execution of monumental works, that facilities for obtaining stone were great and the conditions of the soil more favourable to the preservation of delicate articles. It must be recalled that Egypt was still without wheeled vehicles though she could replace by magic images the living victims immolated in the oldest Sumerian tombs.

Approaching the question in another way, we shall find in the sequel that the majority of European metal types, referable specifically to one or other of the Oriental groups, go back quite unambiguously to prediluvian or Sumerian models. Still most daggers in Western and

Central Europe are inspired by peculiarly Egyptian forms, traceable back to Middle Predynastic times. As all specialized early dynastic forms are confined to Egypt, the diffusion of the dagger type from the Nile must go back to Middle Predynastic times. If Egypt was diffusing metallurgical knowledge so early, the value of the numerical preponderance of diffused Sumerian types as evidence for the *original* centre of metallurgy is weakened. And so the question must be left open.

CHAPTER II

METALLURGY AND TRADE

MINING AND SMELTING

A DETAILED account of the metallurgical processes employed in antiquity must be relegated to technical works, but a short description of some aspects thereof is desirable both to justify the assertions of the first chapter and to make intelligible the sequel. As to mining, we have already remarked that at first weathered surface deposits of ore, even if poor, were exploited. In the case of tin, supplies could be obtained from alluvial deposits by washing as with gold. However, it is certain that even in Europe before the end of the Bronze Age the veins of ore were followed underground by means of shafts and galleries many of which are well preserved in the Austrian Alps[19].

The process of smelting, particularly in the case of surface ores, consisting of oxides, silicates or carbonates—the so-called oxidized ores—was comparatively simple. Heating with carbon (charcoal) suffices to effect the reduction and liberate the metallic copper. In the case of some of the copper ores, found principally in deeper workings, a preliminary roasting may be necessary to produce artificially an oxidized ore. The reduction could be quite well effected in a shallow clay-lined pit such as was used in Japan last century[20]. Ignited charcoal is placed on the floor of the pit, and a conical pile of charcoal and ore in alternate layers is heaped up over it. A blast is applied through a clay nozzle when the mass will be reduced in about an hour. The metal settles to

the bottom of the hole. The slag and unburnt charcoal is thereupon raked off, and the metal dragged out
in lumps when on the point of solidifying. The cakes of
raw metal from European "founders' hoards" display
under the microscope the peculiar structure caused by
breaking the metal when it was thus on the point of
solidifying. In the Tyrol remains of more elaborate
furnaces built into the hillside have been found.

Tin and lead can be obtained by the same methods
though the loss from volatilization is considerable. Lead
ores were probably valued at first for the silver they
contain. To purify the precious metal the process termed
cupellation must have been applied. The silver-lead
amalgam produced by simple reduction is strongly heated
in a blast of air whereby the lead is oxidized, the metallic
silver remaining at the bottom of the furnace or crucible.

For the production of the important alloy, bronze,
two processes were available. The ores of copper and
tin might be smelted together or the two metals fused
together. The former process may have been first employed. In the true Bronze Age, however, the extant
evidence points to a deliberate mixture of the two metals.
Another alloy used in antiquity was electrum, consisting
approximately of two parts gold and one part silver. It
was used in Troy, the Caucasus, Mesopotamia and
Hungary. Since the native gold of Transylvania, Pacto-
lus and elsewhere is strongly argentiferous, electrum
may well be a natural alloy.

The raw metal from the smelters was probably not
generally cast into ingots. The material from the bottom
of the furnaces was rather broken up into cakes of
convenient size before it had set hard. However, ingots
were sometimes at least cast. From Cyprus and Crete
we have a number of ingots of copper, probably Cypriote,

cast in the form of a Minoan double-axe and sometimes
stamped with a character of the Minoan script. Similar
ingots are depicted among the tribute brought to
Eighteenth Dynasty Pharaohs, and one has been found
in Sardinia. In Central Europe copper was apparently
traded in the form of neck-rings or torques. Hoards
consisting exclusively of such torques, made of pure
copper, have been unearthed particularly between the
tin-producing region of Bohemia and the copper lodes
of Slovakia and the Alps[41].

CASTING AND MOULDS

The operations of the smith need more detailed
description to enable us to understand the peculiarities
of the metal objects that constitute such prominent
documents on Bronze Age civilization. The raw metal
was first melted in crucibles of clay. In Egypt these
crucibles, to judge by the tomb paintings, were heated
over an open fire. Actual crucibles have been found in
European sites. But these exhibit the effects of heat
only round the rim[20] and on the inside, so that we must
assume the use of a furnace similar to that employed in
Japan last century. The clay crucible was placed in a
hollow packed with charcoal; sticks of ignited charcoal
were laid upon it and these covered with lumps of
copper. On the application of a blast the metal would
melt and drip into the crucible. In either case a blast
was needed to secure adequate heat so that the smith
must have assistants. In Egypt down to the New Kingdom human lungs provided the current of air, and we
see parties of youths sitting by the furnace and blowing
down pipes! Thereafter leather bellows are depicted. The
wind was conducted into the fire through a clay nozzle.
Such blast pipes are regularly found in European

1

2

3

Fig. 1. (1) Nilotic smith at work.
   (2) Clay nozzle from pile-village of Mörigen, Switzerland (after Ischer).
   (3) Egyptian goldsmiths (after de Morgan).

villages of the Late Bronze Age, notably the Swiss lake-dwellings(100), Velem Szent Vid and other industrial settlements in Hungary (Fig. 1, no. 2).

Simple objects, flat on one face, can be cast by pouring the molten metal into a form, hollowed out in the ground or carved on a block of stone(5). This is known as the open hearth process. A number of stone moulds for casting simple objects such as flat celts have been found in Great Britain and other countries. Moulds for flat celts are peculiarly common in Scotland (Fig. 2, no. 1).

Usually a more elaborate sort of mould was required. Even for daggers (except the most primitive flat type), spear-heads and palstaves a mould in at least two pieces must be employed(5). A number of specimens have come down to us from the Middle and Late Bronze Age of Europe (Fig. 2, no. 2). The usual procedure was to take two corresponding pieces of stone, generally schist or sandstone, carefully rubbed flat and smooth on one face each, and to carve on each piece the negative outline of half the desired object. By combining the two a "valve mould" is obtained whose internal hollow is the exact negative of the object to be manufactured. Of course it is essential to secure an exact correspondence between the two valves and a stable union. That might be ensured by dowelling the two halves together, but often it was thought sufficient just to lash the two pieces together; ribs are sometimes cut in the back of the mould to give the thongs a better purchase.

When the valves have been fitted together liquid metal is poured in through a channel with a funnel-like mouth, specially cut for it in the mould. At least in the case of large objects, like rapier blades, fine capillaries running from the internal hollow to the edge must be cut to allow the air to escape from the enclosed space.

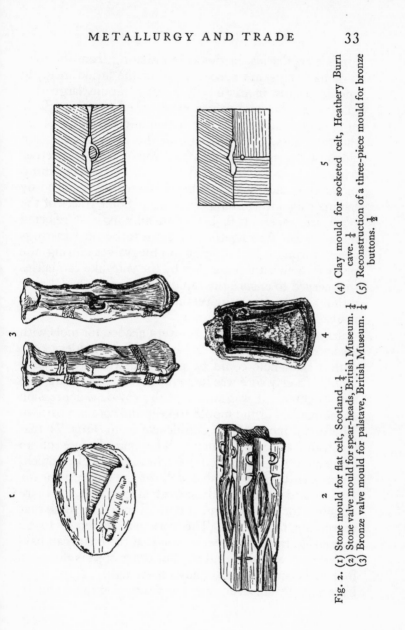

Fig. 2. (1) Stone mould for flat celt, Scotland. ¼
(2) Stone valve mould for spear-heads, British Museum. ¼
(3) Bronze valve mould for palstave, British Museum. ¼
(4) Clay mould for socketed celt, Heathery Burn cave. ¼
(5) Reconstruction of a three-piece mould for bronze buttons. ½

Similar capillaries, in this case radiating from the inlet tube like veins, are needed to allow the liquid metal to spread evenly in casting in a valve mould large thin plates. As the two valves never fitted exactly, a little of the liquid metal will have spread into the join between the two faces. This appears on the product as a thin ridge or "seam" (Gussnaht) all round which, together with the spur or "fount" left by the metal remaining in the inlet channel, must be subsequently removed by hammering and rubbing with sand. Some traces of the seam are generally to be found on rough or rejected metal tools. Among the latter are to be seen castings spoilt through the slipping of the valves during the process. The little ridges left by the vein-like capillaries that served to ensure the rapid spread of the metal over a thin surface might be retained as decorative elements instead of being rubbed away.

More complicated moulds were needed for tools with a socket for the shaft. Axe-heads of the modern type with a shaft-hole could be produced with a two-valve mould if a clay core was introduced where the shaft-hole was to come. It was sufficient to provide a depression at the bottom of the mould to keep the core in position. There is a mould for a double-axe from Troy VI that illustrates the arrangement. The manufacture of an implement like a socketed spear-head or a socketed celt, where the tube for the shaft follows the long axis of the artifact and is essentially closed at one end, is more difficult; for the metal must flow all round the core that represents the socket. The core has therefore to be suspended from its upper end so that the metal can pass under it as well as round it. For other objects three- or four-piece moulds must have been used. None such have actually survived, but the position of the seams or flaws due to the slipping of one part of the mould show how the several valves were arranged. Looped buttons can be cast in a tripartite mould, one piece containing the negative of the button top while two pieces with the join at right angles to the face of the first section provided the loop (Fig. 2, no. 5). Chains composed of closed annular links required four valves joining obliquely.

Nevertheless, except for quite simple implements, stone or metal moulds were seldom used for the actual casting. This was carried out rather by the *cire perdue* (verlorener Form) process. The procedure is as follows. A wax model of the desired object is first prepared. This is then dipped in a bath of clay of creamy consistency so that it becomes coated all over with an exactly fitting skin of clay which is allowed to dry on it. The whole is then enveloped in thicker clay to protect it. When this too has dried, the whole is heated so that the wax melts and runs out through an aperture left for the purpose. Liquid metal is poured by the same channel into the vacuum created. When the metal has cooled, the clay of the mould must of course be broken to allow of the extraction of the casting. Each mould can thus serve for one casting only. Hence the archaeological evidence for the use of the process in prehistoric times is mainly inferential. Only a few fragments of the actual moulds have survived. But one group of objects, representing the stock-in-trade of a Late Bronze Age smith unearthed at St Chély-du-Tarn (Lozère) in France, included a large lump of wax[4]. From Egypt and Mesopotamia textual evidence for the employment of the *cire perdue* process is extant.

The *cire perdue* process sounds very complicated and laborious. But really, once the technique has been acquired, the only part that required time and close attention was the preparation of the wax model. This could be greatly accelerated and simplified by casting the model in a mould. In point of fact, while some stone moulds of the types just described above were no doubt directly employed for making the final bronze casting, the majority of them, and probably all bronze moulds (Fig. 2, no. 3), were used not for the casting proper but for forming quickly the wax model. Models could be turned out very readily with the aid of such moulds and moreover could very easily be trimmed up and embellished so as to yield an admirable model. Difficult operations could be simplified by the use of this procedure since the model was always subject to adjustment before being coated with clay. So, in the manufacture of socketed celts, the core could be steadied during the casting of the model by a wedge under its lower end; the crack in the wax left by this could easily be filled up before the model was dipped in its clay bath. It is possible too that the marvellous curvilinear patterns that adorn Hungarian and Scandinavian bronzes were engraved, not with hammer and chisel on the hard bronze itself, but on the soft wax of the model.

The *cire perdue* process is also applicable to the casting of thin objects over a core. Metal vessels can be made by modelling a lump of clay to the required shape, coating the lump with a thin layer of wax and then enveloping the whole in a mantle of clay, leaving of course in the outer cover a passage for drawing off the wax and pouring in the metal. In the case of objects such as vases the clay core would be broken up after the casting, but in other cases it might be left in place. The Scottish National Museum possesses a sword-pommel which turns out on examination to be just a clay core sheathed in thin bronze. It was doubtless prepared in the way just described.

Castings made on the open hearth or in a valve mould had subsequently to be trimmed up by rubbing with sand and hammering to remove the seam and other roughnesses. The edge of cutting tools and weapons, whether cast in stone moulds or by the *cire perdue* process, must be sharpened by hammering which served also to harden the metal. Hammering was moreover the only method of producing sheet-metal known to the ancients. It must be remembered that while copper and gold can be worked with the hammer while cold, bronze must be brought to a red heat before hammering has much effect.

Wire, at least in Europe, was never made by "drawing". Gold and bronze wire of a round section might be made by hammering out a rod of the metal and then rolling it to round off the edges. Alternatively a narrow ribbon of thin metal was twisted very tightly. A wire of triangular cross-section might be made by hammering a metal rod into a V-shaped groove. In Egypt there is some evidence that gold wire was really manufactured under the Middle Kingdom by drawing—forcing the metal through fine holes.

For joining pieces of metal, rivets were used throughout the Bronze Age, as to-day. The rivets had, of course, to be of softer metal than the objects to be riveted, e.g. a bronze poor in tin. In the Aegean and Spain silver rivets were often employed for riveting bronze or copper daggers. In the Ancient East soldering was also regularly used for joining pieces of gold and silver. The Sumerians also employed lead as a solder for copper. In barbarian Europe no such processes were known during the Bronze Age. That incidentally debarred the

European jeweller from using filigree work, gold wire soldered on to a solid background so as to form a pattern, a process very popular with Sumerian and Trojan gold-smiths. Brazing, the union of two pieces by heating the edges to be joined nearly to melting-point and hammering, is also said to have been practised by the Sumerians and was possibly known even to the barbarians of continental Europe. The latter certainly employed a process of casting-on (Anguss). When, for example, it was desired to weld together two tubes, they were placed end to end and the join surrounded by a wax ring. This was then coated with clay and replaced by a metal ring by the *cire perdue* process. The hilts of daggers were sometimes cast to fit on to the blades in the same way, the hilts being modelled in wax fitting over the blades.

TRADE IN THE ANCIENT EAST

A *sine qua non* for the free use of metal whether on the alluvial plains of Mesopotamia or on the boulder clays of Denmark was, as we saw, regular foreign trade. In the Ancient East trade by the third millennium B.C. was probably conducted on very much the same lines as native commerce in Asia to-day, save that coined money was unknown. A collection of clay tablets found in Cappadocia are inscribed with the business letters of a group of bankers and merchants settled there in connection with the metal trade. They give a lively picture of the traffic between the metalliferous regions of Asia Minor and the agricultural and industrial cities of the Tigris-Euphrates plains. Great caravans of merchandise travelled up and down the famous route that follows the Euphrates. The commerce was financed by a system of loans, secured by contracts many of which have come down to us. Other documents from Mesopotamia, also written in the wedge-like characters called cuneiform, refer to the importation of copper from the mountainous region east of the Tigris and of metal and stone from Magan (probably Oman on the Persian Gulf). Egyptian records from the Old Kingdom onwards refer to expeditions sent by the Pharaohs across the desert to Sinai for the extraction of copper and turquoise. Contemporary inscriptions mention the importation of cedar-wood by ship from North Syria. It was to secure this trade that the Egyptians established a colony or protectorate at Byblos. Sidney Smith(7) has pointed out how commercial relations between the civilized States would have involved actual transference of population as they do to-day. Craftsmen from foreign lands would gravitate to cities where political or geographical circumstances had created a market for their wares and skill and would in turn add to the riches of their adopted home.

Archaeological data faithfully reflect these commercial relations by the wide distribution of rare substances or common types. Lapis lazuli beads were worn even in prehistoric times from Baluchistan to Egypt. Obsidian was used in the prediluvian settlements of Susa and al'Ubaid as in predynastic Egypt. In Late Predynastic and protodynastic times we find a number of artistic motives and architectural devices, at all times common in Mesopotamia, abruptly and temporarily adopted in Egypt as if in imitation of Sumerian originals. Conversely in the early Royal Tombs of Ur we find the Egyptian sistrum represented. The most dramatic proof of extensive commercial relations is however the discovery in several pre-Sargonic sites in Mesopotamia of seals, differing altogether in design and fabric from the countless native seals, but identical with specimens unearthed in prehistoric sites in the Indus valley. This is the earliest recorded instance of the transmission of manufactures over such vast distances. The transference of such instruments of commercial negotiation clearly implies an extensive trade in other articles, such as cotton, between the two distant regions. And so we see that the caravans were already crossing the Syrian and Persian deserts and merchantmen already furrowing the Mediterranean and Erythraean Seas five thousand years ago!

BRONZE AGE TRADE IN EUROPE

The conditions of trade in barbarian Europe would naturally be somewhat different. Here there were as yet no cities, but only villages of peasant farmers or meeting-places for semi-nomadic herdsmen. While such had little but slaves to offer the civilized folk of the Ancient East, the tin of Tuscany and Cornwall, the gold of Transylvania and Ireland and above all the amber of Jutland and East Prussia[23] might well find a market in the East Mediterranean world. It is signifi-cant that the first continental centres where metal came into use lie either in the vicinity of such deposits or along routes leading thereto. Relations with the East Mediterranean centres of metallurgy are demonstrated not only by the obvious derivation of most early Euro-pean metal objects from ancient Oriental models, but also by their association with Egyptian or Aegean manufactures such as glazed beads or, in Central Europe, Mediterranean shells.

The intimacy and wide extent of commercial relations between the several parts of Europe during the Bronze Age is illustrated by the number of types common to a wide area and by the diffusion of stray examples of types,

specialized in a particular area, far beyond their primary
habitat. Thus at the beginning of the Bronze Age the
same types of dagger were in use in Eastern Spain,
Brittany, Great Britain, Upper Italy, Czechoslovakia,
Southern Germany and Eastern France. The peculiar
weapon known as the halberd (p. 79) was common to
Upper Italy, Spain, Ireland and Central Germany.
Direct interchange of goods is demonstrated by the
occurrence sporadically in Wales, Cornwall, Brittany,
Central Germany and Denmark of a type of gold col-
lar, termed a lunula, common only in Ireland and
Scotland(57). Again a form of battle-axe, native to Hun-
gary, is represented by stray specimens from Bavaria,
Mecklenburg-Strelitz, Silesia, Poland, and the Uk-
raine. Axe-heads of types characteristic of Britain and
Italy respectively have been found side by side in
Sweden.

It is therefore plain that even manufactured articles
were traded between the various communities of European barbarians, to say nothing of substances like amber
and jet. But it must be noted that the "communities"
just referred to are more than geographical districts, and
the "types" that help to define them have other func-
tions to fulfil in the archaeologist's scheme. We must
therefore diverge here to define a "culture".

DEFINITION OF A CULTURE

During the Bronze Age, as in the preceding period,
Europe was divided up among a multiplicity of distinct
communities or peoples. These may be distinguished
from one another by burial rites, architecture, art and
the types of tools, weapons, vessels and ornaments they
used. The distinctive metal, bone, stone and pottery

types (artifacts), regularly found associated[1] in graves
and settlements over a given geographical area, together
with the peculiarities of the domestic and funerary
structures in which they occur, constitute what is called
a culture. In a culture thus defined there is good reason
to recognize the material expression of that community
of traditions which distinguishes a people in the modern
sense.

Types, therefore, are symbols of cultural groups and
their relations, but also, as we shall see, indicators of
relative age. This dual function is not without incon-
venience; for a culture, like the people it represents, is
not static but can move about. It is therefore well to
ask in any given case whether the appearance of a
specific type in a region outside its original home is due
to trade or migration. In the first case its appearance in
the new region will serve to establish a synchronism
with the home area; in the alternative this is not guaran-
teed; for a conservative people coming into a progressive
area may bring with them and retain old-fashioned types.

To answer the question the following considerations
are helpful. When a culture moves bodily, i.e. when
the whole complex of types, fashions and habits spreads,
into an area where the said forms of tools and weapons,
artistic conventions and burial rites had not previously
been generally current, we must admit that we are
dealing with a migration. That might conceivably be a
slow process throughout which some or all the types
remained without material modification. In any case,
the more intimate and imponderable traits of a culture,
such as pottery and burial rites that could hardly be

[1] Objects are said to be associated when they are found together
in circumstances indicative of contemporary use, e.g. as the furniture of a
single burial or in the ruins of a single hut.

traded and would rarely be imitated and that only by immediate neighbours, will move as much as portable commodities like metal types. The reader will, moreover, doubtless concede that the supersession of a more practical type, like the shaft-hole axe, by an inferior one, such as the socketed celt, can hardly be explained by the external relation of trade or neighbourly imitation but implies something deeper such as conquest or immigration.

Conversely when stray objects properly belonging to one culture are found in the area of another associated with types proper to the latter, we are dealing with "external relations". Trade is the simplest and most natural explanation for the appearance of a Hungarian axe in North Germany or an Irish ornament in Denmark, but it is always possible that the axe was dropped by a Hungarian raider or the lunula looted from Ireland by a Danish pirate.

HOARDS

As a result of the extensive trade of the Bronze Age and its peculiar conditions, we have a class of closed finds very rare in previous epochs. In addition to grave furniture and relics from settlements we now encounter what are called "hoards"(4). These are groups of implements, ornaments or vessels buried together in the earth. Sometimes hoards have been enclosed in a vessel; occasionally there are traces of a sack or leather bag, but naturally such receptacles have seldom survived. Hoards are of various kinds: some appear to be just the personal possessions of an individual or a household and may be termed "domestic hoards". Such consist of a few tools, weapons and ornaments, comprising as a rule only one specimen of each type and normally showing signs of use. They have probably been buried by their owner in time of danger or while he was travelling and never retrieved so that their survival is an indication of the owner's misfortune. Domestic hoards may be regarded as closed finds guaranteeing the contemporary use of all the articles deposited together. They are thus valuable for synchronizing types, but otherwise of no special interest.

Objects found together at the foot of a rock or a tree or in a spring or a swamp, may sometimes at least represent offerings made to a divinity supposed to inhabit the spot(81). They are accordingly termed "votive hoards" and in general provide no guarantee of the contemporary use of the objects comprised in them.

The remaining hoards belong to traders and normally contain several examples of each type of tool, weapon or ornament. In the Early Bronze Age the traders' hoards consist almost entirely of new or half-finished articles. Some at least seem to have belonged to travelling tinkers, bartering metal products which they were prepared to finish off on the spot to suit the taste of the customer. So some Central German hoards contain a number of dagger- or halberd-blades to which the merchant would fit hilts as required. The same hoards often contain amber beads, showing that their depositors were engaged in the amber trade. In the Late Bronze Age some of the traders had begun to specialize in particular lines, and accordingly we find hoards consisting exclusively of swords, sickles, or vases as the case may be. But even in the Early Bronze Age there are hoards composed entirely of ingots of raw copper in the form of torques.

The contents of the foregoing commercial hoards in all probability were in contemporary use. That is not, however, true of another group of hoards, very common in the Late Bronze Age, that seem in some cases to have been left by a class of trader. They are characterized by the presence of old and broken tools, obviously scrap metal collected for remelting, and often too of metallurgical tools, moulds and ingots of raw metal; such are termed "founders' hoards" to distinguish them from ordinary traders' hoards. The distinction is vital since the objects included in them may be of very different date, being in fact any old pieces of scrap metal. Yet some such hoards probably belong to gangs of travelling tinkers who went round the countryside repairing broken tools and collecting scrap metal at a time when the demand was peculiarly intense. Others are so large that they must represent the stock of a village smithy buried at a moment of danger or of a station in the international metal trade.

The accepted explanation of traders' hoards is that they were buried by the travelling merchant, when he saw himself threatened by some danger, with the intention of reclaiming them when the peril was past. And in point of fact when plotted on a map, they are seen to lie along natural routes and to be thickest just where danger might be expected, for instance on the frontier of two cultural provinces. Hence a multitude of hoards, whether commercial or domestic, is anything but a sign of prosperity. It was rather in times of unrest that valuables had to be entrusted to the preservation of the earth. So the majority of hoards of Roman coins, unearthed in France and Scotland, are shown by their dates to have been buried during reigns when it is known that those lands were harried by civil war or barbarian raids.

TRADE ROUTES

With the aid of maps showing the distribution of contemporary hoards and of individual types, found isolated or in other closed finds, it is possible to plot out in some detail the main arteries of the European economic system. Of all the commercial highways thus disclosed, the amber route (23) connecting the Baltic and the Adriatic was the most important. The ways, that diverged slightly at different periods, are clearly marked by amber ornaments, datable by their associations in graves and hoards. From Jutland the fossil resin was transmitted, during the Early Bronze Age, up the Elbe to Bohemia and thence across the Böhmer Wald to the Upper Danube at Linz or Passau. An early branch route, however, followed the Saale valley through Thuringia (where there are important salt deposits) to the head-waters of the Main and then reached the Upper Danube over the Frankish Jura. Thence in either case the Inn was followed to the foot of the Brenner. The traders used this pass to bring their goods by way of the Adige to the Po valley and the head of the Adriatic.

The large number of tools and weapons of Italian pattern found along the amber route show that the inhabitants of Upper Italy played an important part as intermediaries in the trade. Still the quantities of amber found in tombs in Greece from 1600 B.C. on leave no doubt that the Aegean market was already open. At the same time Bohemia was a very important agency, so much so indeed that its inhabitants may be said to have controlled the northern end of the route. The principal medium of barter used in the actual vicinity of the deposits during the Early Bronze Age was a gold ear-ring or lock-ring of a type originating immediately in

Hungary and perhaps made of Hungarian gold; such ornaments have been found in very considerable numbers in Jutland as well as in Bohemia and Saxo-Thuringia. It looks as if the people of the last two regions kept to themselves the bronze work of the South and bartered to the Danish natives only the gold they got from Hungary in exchange for tin.

During the Middle Bronze Age the western branch of the central amber route along the Saale came into greater prominence, and a loop way was introduced as an alternative, following an old hill trackway across Thuringia to the Rhine near Mainz, then running upstream to the mouth of the Neckar, and traversing that gap to reach the Upper Danube near Augsburg.

Very possibly the East Prussian amber deposits were being tapped even during the Early Bronze Age. A series of hoards and stray bronzes, mostly of Saxo-Thuringian pattern, can be traced across Eastern Germany and Poland to converge near the mouth of the Vistula. Though the hoards of this date do not contain amber, they clearly denote a trade in Saxo-Thuringian bronzes which can only have been exchanged for East Prussian amber. The regular and extensive exploitation of the latter deposits, however, dates only from a late phase of the local Bronze Age, overlapping with the Early Iron Age in Austria. At that date the material was carried up the Vistula to its first elbow at Torun, thence to the Oder near Glogau and so across Silesia to the Glatz Pass. Thence the March valley was followed to the Danube. Thereafter the exact course of the route is obscure, but it seems to have traversed Styria and Carniola to reach the head of the Adriatic.

Other routes on a smaller scale have been worked out in limited areas. A glance at the map of hoards, classified by periods appended to Behrens' *Bronzezeit Süddeutschlands*, will give a good idea of what can be determined. On the other hand, the map of hoards in Déchelette's *Manuel* tells one very little, because all hoards are shown by the same symbol without distinction of age.

THE CLIMATE OF THE BRONZE AGE

Intercourse during the Bronze Age was facilitated by the climatic conditions then ruling over our continent[24]. While the earlier part of the New Stone Age had been wetter, though warmer, than the present, drier conditions set in towards the close of that period and were intensified during the Bronze Age. The result of this sub-boreal phase, as climatologists term it, was that tracts that are to-day naturally wooded became parklands or, in extreme cases, open heath or steppe[25]. As the primeval forest, dangerous to traverse by reason of the bears and wolves it sheltered, and difficult to clear with expensive bronze axes, presented to our forefathers the most serious obstacle to settlement and free movement, the dry period was to most Europeans a climatic optimum. In some parts of the North European plain, however, the drought may have been so great as to be incompatible with sedentary agriculture, thus promoting popular migrations. In Ireland and large tracts of Great Britain, on the contrary, it is excessive wind and moisture that impedes the growth of timber. Here, therefore, the sub-boreal epoch was certainly a forest phase; to it belongs the upper layer (there is often an older one of Mesolithic Age) of tree trunks and stools discovered in our peat-mosses. In these islands, therefore, the sub-boreal dryness had little effect upon the area available for settlement. Only the dry uplands were really thickly populated, and even the trade routes avoided as far as possible the wooded valleys unless a navigable river flowed along them.

VEHICLES AND SHIPS

The commercial intercourse, essential to the very existence of a Bronze Age, was expedited by a series of inventions. Perhaps the most revolutionary was the harnessing of animal motive power, the first step in the emancipation of mankind from the burden of crushing physical labour that has led to the steam engine and the petrol motor. Neolithic man possessed oxen and other tame beasts, but there is no conclusive evidence that he ever set them even to drag his plough; when he travelled he and his wife must carry the household goods as among the Australian aborigines to-day. But very early in the Bronze Age of the Ancient East the ox had been yoked to the plough and set to work in the fields, and even in Europe, by an early phase of the same period, representations of an ox-drawn plough were being carved on the rocks of the Ligurian Alps.

On sandy deserts or open grass-lands the same animal could be harnessed to draw loads on runners.[1] Effective use of the animal's tractive powers, however, involved the discovery of the wheel. Therewith mankind set foot on the road that led to the motor car. The earliest wheeled vehicles known as yet have recently been brought to light in tombs at Kish and Ur dating from before 3000 B.C.[8]. The wheels are clumsy affairs, just three solid pieces of wood, shaped to segments of a circle, clamped together and tyred with leather, that

[1] There is some very uncertain evidence from Finland for the use of a sleigh, drawn presumably by reindeer or dogs, even in Mesolithic times.

turned with the axle. Otherwise the main outlines of
later cars are clearly foreshadowed. The draught animals,
asses or oxen, were harnessed on either side of a pole
fixed to the middle of the fore axle. They were guided
by reins which passed through a double ring or terret,
fixed to the chariot pole. Light two-wheeled chariots
are little, if at all, later than these four-wheeled carts. A
model cart from the Indus valley dates from the third
millennium, while by that time wheeled vehicles were also
known in Crete, as is shown by a clay model of M.M. I
date. Even in Spain there are quaint rock-paintings,
representing a wheeled cart, that may date back to the
Copper Age. In Egypt, however, wheeled vehicles
were apparently unknown before the end of the Middle
Kingdom. Thereafter they were introduced by the barbarian invaders known as the Hyksôs. About the same
time the two-wheeled chariot drawn by horses was
adopted in the Aegean area. In the Minoan and Mycenaean chariots the axle is under the body of the car,
whereas in contemporary Egyptian vehicles it was in
front(26). Whether wheeled vehicles were known north
of the Alps during the earlier part of the Bronze Age
is still uncertain. By the middle of that period bridle-
bits furnish, as we shall see, evidence of the subjugation
of the horse, and pendants in the form of a wheel imply
a knowledge of that device.

While on the topic of the wheel we must mention
another very different application of the invention, the
potter's wheel(27). All Neolithic vessels have been built
up by hand, aided only by a leaf or mat on which the
lump of clay might stand, and smoothing tools of wood
or bone. By Old Kingdom times, however, the Egyptians were utilizing a pivoted disc that would revolve
readily as the pot was being shaped. It is sometimes

called the *tournette*. But by 3000 B.C. Sumerian potters
were already using the true wheel that will spin fast.
The lump of soft clay is placed on the centre of, or on
a tray connected by a sort of axle to the centre of, a
horizontal wheel. The latter can be made to rotate
rapidly by the potter's foot or by an assistant. A lump
of clay of the proper consistency thus set spinning almost
automatically assumes a cylindrical form; all the potter's
hand has to do is to give the gyrating mass the required
contours. By the use of this device ten or twenty vessels
can be modelled, and that more symmetrically, in the
time required for building up one by free hand. On
the other hand, with the adoption of the wheel, pottery
tends to become a factory product and to lose much of
its individuality.

Going back in the East to at least 3000 B.C., the
potter's wheel reached Crete and Troy II by M.M. I
times (from which dates the earliest evidence too for
the wheeled vehicle in the Aegean). Soon after the
device crossed to mainland Greece. But farther north
and west pots continued to be made exclusively by the
free hand till late in the Iron Age. There is, however,
evidence that a cognate device, the lathe, was in use in
Britain by the middle of the local Bronze Age (see p. 189).

Parallel to the acceleration of land transport by the
use of the wheel went a great expansion of maritime
intercourse. Even Mesolithic man had been able to
venture on the sea in some sort of craft so as to reach
the island of Oransay, and the immense voyages of the
Polynesians in improved (top-straked) dug-outs, show
what could be accomplished without the use of any
metal tool. But no true ships certainly antedate the
copper axe and chisel. Even before the union of the
lands in one kingdom, the predynastic Egyptians

depicted on their vases quite big vessels with two cabins and propelled by as many as fifty oars. These boats seem to have grown out of a small raft made of bundles of papyrus lashed together, but their sides were probably already made of planks of Syrian timber tied together like the original papyrus bundles. At the same time another type of vessel with a very high prow, only known at first from Egyptian monuments, had grown up on the Persian Gulf and the Erythraean Sea(10). These were sailing ships, so that the dwellers on those coasts had already harnessed the winds as their contemporaries on shore had subdued the strength of ox and ass. This is another mechanical invention attributable to the Bronze Age.

In the Aegean(12), ships, related to the high-prowed Erythraean type but equipped with fixed rudders, are depicted from Early Minoan times onwards. Probably it was hence that hardy mariners sailed beyond the Pillars of Hercules whose ships provided the models for Scandinavian boat-builders. The latters' products have been depicted on rock-carvings in Southern Sweden. In any case the Egyptian, Aegean and Syrian ships of the third millennium were certainly capable of crossing the Mediterranean. The diffusion of megalithic tombs along the coasts of Portugal, France, Ireland and Scotland to Scandinavia may reasonably be regarded as proof that they also faced the Atlantic and the North Sea. And indeed Danish amber and English jet were reaching the western coasts of the Mediterranean even during the Copper Age. So it is fairly certain that maritime intercourse between Scandinavia, the British Isles and the Iberian Peninsula supplemented the great transcontinental land route from the North to the Mediterranean throughout the Bronze Age.

WRITING, WEIGHTS AND MEASURES

The other inventions incidental to international commerce need not be described here in detail. The necessity for contracts and accounts no doubt gave an impetus to the development of writing. Many documents written on clay tablets from Mesopotamia and Crete bear witness to this use of writing. As mastery of the art was the accomplishment of a few "scribes", the average correspondent, being unable to sign his name, would instead impress upon the soft clay a seal bearing a distinctive emblem, originally perhaps his guardian animal or totem.

A system of metrology was equally needed for trade. Various standards were used by the different civilizations of the Ancient East. In continental Europe have been found a number of symbolic double-axes, apparently Copper or Early Bronze Age in date. On being placed on the scales, it is found that the weights of such are interrelated, all being multiples of an Asiatic unit termed the *mina*. Late in the Bronze Age weights of stone and lead have been found in the Swiss lake-dwellings. In form they are quite like modern weights with a little loop for suspension; they too correspond to multiples of a *mina*(4).

TYPOLOGICAL CHRONOLOGY

The intimacy of the subsisting commercial relations makes the correlation and synchronization of deposits from different parts of Europe far easier during the Bronze Age than in the preceding New Stone Age. The types of tools, weapons and ornaments, current in our continent, did not remain constant for any length of time as they had in the Orient. They were rapidly modified in response to new inventions and changes of fashion. In the case of some tools and weapons the changes take place in a continuous and regular order in one direction, illustrating progressive advances, just as improvements are incorporated in each year's new model of, say, an Austin car. Thus the celts or axe-heads are modified along several divergent lines till all converge again upon the socketed celt. Similarly the triangular dagger grows into a short dirk, then a rapier and eventually a cut-and-thrust sword.

When the progressive improvement of a tool can thus be represented as a series of stages, we have what is termed a "typological series"[28]. The presumption is that the more perfect types are later than the cruder ones, so that such a series would have a direct chronological value. This assumption is not, however, necessarily justified; for degeneration is as much a fact as evolution. A typological series can only be accepted as representing a chronological sequence when the direction of evolution has been tested by the independent dating of at least two stages. Moreover, the more rudimentary types naturally tend to persist side by side with their descendants. Hence while an advanced type indicates a relatively late date, a more rudimentary one is no such sure sign of antiquity. If you see a 1930 model Austin in a garage, you are sure that the year is 1930 or later; a 1924 model is no sure proof that you have been transported back to that year.

In several parts of continental Europe it has been possible to construct typological series illustrating the development of the celt, the dagger and sword, the spear-head, the razor, the safety-pin, etc., and to synchronize the several stages in one series with corresponding stages in the rest. This gives a sequence of periods defined by contemporary types. Montelius, a Swede, who first elaborated this method of establishing the relative chronology of barbarian Europe, recognized six periods in Scandinavia. It is claimed that in a large number of closed finds[1] of say Period III, only a small minority of the types would belong to Periods II or IV and none at all to I or V.

Within the area served by European trade the several stages, distinguished typologically in the different provinces, can be synchronized, and we thus obtain a relative chronology, based on typology, valid for the whole of Europe. On these principles we can easily distinguish everywhere within the economic system three main periods which we term the Early, Middle and Late Bronze Ages. The last period should close with the beginning of the first Iron Age or Hallstatt period in Austria, Switzerland and South Germany, but actually in Great Britain, Scandinavia and Hungary the arrival of iron was belated so that we have a prolongation of the Bronze Age in such areas.

While the tripartite division above indicated is accurate enough for the present study and is indeed as minute as can be applied in practice to Europe as a whole, much finer divisions have been established by local specialists for restricted areas. Montelius, as noted, distinguished six periods for Scandinavia (generally represented by Roman numerals) of which the last three overlap with the Hallstatt Iron Age farther south. Sophus Müller[29] identified twice as many in Denmark. P. Reinecke[30] divides the pure Bronze Age in South Germany into four periods, lettered A to D, followed by

[1] See note on p. 42.

a phase he terms Hallstatt A, in which iron had never-theless not penetrated beyond the Alps. Kraft(43), who follows Reinecke, therefore terms his Hallstatt A "Bronze Age E". The Early and Late Bronze Ages of Britain were each divided into two periods by Montelius(59), giving five in all. British archaeologists are, however, agreed that this subdivision cannot be carried through in practice and have further observed that the first marked gap in our Bronze Age comes at the beginning of what should be the Late Bronze Age(55); the Middle period is with us always vague and ill-defined. In France Déchelette(4) distinguished four periods, but these[1] are discordant with Reinecke's Central European system which, for reasons explained below, must set the standard.

Any typological division is necessarily somewhat arbitrary and must be used with due caution. It is plainly applicable only to regions forming part of a single economic system, so that the interchange of goods and the spread of ideas is rapid and regular. The systems upon which our tripartite division is based were devised for countries lying along the central amber trade route (p. 46) where most of the leading types were evolved. We shall meet serious difficulties in applying it to other regions, such as England, which participated only in-directly or not at all in Scandinavian, Central European and North Italian progress. In the case of Spain, relations with the rest of continental Europe seem to have been broken off during the Early Bronze Age, and types of the Middle period are totally lacking. It is, therefore, likely that Early Bronze Age types remained

[1] On his Plate III (Period III) 1 and 10 are Reinecke B, and 2, 5, 11, 14, 16, 19 and 20 Reinecke C, therefore all Middle Bronze Age; while 3, 6, 7, 8, 9, 13 and 15 are Late Bronze Age, Reinecke D.

current in the Peninsula long after they had gone out of fashion in Central Europe. Trade between Western Europe and Russia only became effective in the latest Bronze Age. All the older types are virtually absent, but that by no means implies that the vast area was depopulated from the end of the Stone Age. Similarly only a few celts and daggers of Early Bronze Age type are known from Denmark because there a belated Stone Age persisted. One or two little ornaments of Early Bronze Age type from late Stone Age graves demonstrate this overlap(3).

Again a type, not clearly imported and datable in its place of origin, can only be invoked as dating a deposit if the type in question was in effective use, and so susceptible of evolutionary modification, in the culture to which the deposit belongs. For example, in Hungary "celts" were seldom used for axe-heads, the normal axe-head having a hole for the shaft as in our modern tool. Accordingly the celt in Hungary was never improved as in other parts of Europe by the growth of flanges, wings, and then a stop-ridge. The flat celt remained in vogue, but its occurrence here is no indication of an Early Bronze Age date.

A further defect of typological chronology is the difficulty of recognizing what may be called "retardation", when synchronizing different provinces. On the theory, each improvement in the typological series originated at one point and quickly spread thence throughout the economic system. But there is no guarantee that the new type should be traded in all directions or find immediate acceptance everywhere. On a rigid application of the typological method all deposits containing types belonging to the same phase should be contemporary. Yet there are indications that the Late Bronze Age types evolved in Central Europe (Upper Italy, Czechoslovakia, and Southern Germany) were only introduced into Britain and Hungary as the result of migrations that may have been quite gradual. Yet the scheme offers no means of checking the possible delay thus involved.

ABSOLUTE CHRONOLOGY

The foundation of the European Bronze Age in, and its continued connections with, the Aegean and the Ancient East, opens up the possibility of assigning to the relative divisions sketched above absolute values in terms of solar years. The invention of the Oriental prototypes from which the European objects are ultimately derived plainly gives a *terminus post quem* for the appearance of the latter. The range of the simpler original forms, such as flat celts, is, however, so great as to afford no serviceable basis for synchronisms. The earliest pins, ear-rings and collars current in the Danubian province reproduce exactly specialized Asiatic models. But the first two groups go back in their homeland to before 3000 B.C., which is an impossible date for the European copies. The collars on the other hand are known from Syria and Egypt first about 1800 B.C., and this, if the Oriental origin of the form be admitted, would give a reasonable upper limit for our Early Bronze Age. An approximation to a lower limit is suggested by a clay vessel from an Early Bronze Age grave in Saxony that seems to copy a peculiar sort of metal cup popular in the Aegean between 1700 and 1500 B.C. Certain Egyptian or Cretan paste beads found in tombs furnished with Early Bronze Age daggers and axes in South-eastern Spain would give a still lower limit to the period there but that the types of bead have rather too wide a range.

Right at the end of the Middle Bronze Age a rapier of Aegean type, datable there about 1350 B.C., appears in German graves. Then, before 1200, swords, apparently of European origin and Late Bronze Age date, reached Greece and Egypt. A cross-dating is thereby obtained fixing the beginning of the Late Bronze Age between 1300 and 1250 B.C. These figures are, however, only valid for the standard region along the central amber trade route. Elsewhere we must allow for a considerable retardation as already explained.

Knee-shaft of wood for hafting
celts, cf. p. 61.

CHAPTER III

TYPOLOGY

THE variety of tools, weapons, vessels and ornaments at the disposal of Bronze Age man was immensely greater than that known to his Stone Age forebears. It is the material expression of enrichment of life and extended control over nature. The enormous wealth of objects that have come down to us from this brief episode in human history renders possible a vivid picture of that phase of life. Still it is almost embarrassing to the archaeologist. Here we shall describe only the principal types of general interest, confining ourselves in the case of the Ancient East to varieties that have a special chronological or comparative value for students in North-western Europe.

CELTS (AXE-HEADS)

The most widespread, and for typological chronology the most important, family of tools is conveniently termed "celt". This designation is properly applied to axe-heads, but is sometimes extended to adzes and even chisels of comparable form. The celt, whether used as an axe or an adze, was mounted on a wooden staff or shaft, the blade in the former case running parallel to the length of the shaft, in the latter at right angles thereto. The butt might of course be fitted directly into a slit in a straight shaft, but, in the case of all the European celts whose evolution is sketched below, it is certain that the so-called knee-shaft was employed(2). This can most readily be obtained by cutting of a suitable bough or sapling just below the point where a branch grew out of it. This side branch was then broken off a couple of inches from its root and split. The celt was inserted in the cleft which was then bound round with sinews or wire. (Fig. on p. 59.)

Axe-heads and adze-heads of ground stone or flint had been in use throughout the Neolithic Age and indeed formed the most distinctive external trait of that epoch. The earlier metal celts very closely resemble the stone implements, some even reproducing the local peculiarities of the Neolithic celts from the same district. Nevertheless, some authors consider that polished stone celts are all really imitations of copper originals.

The simplest form of metal celt, therefore termed the flat celt, is in any case, like the stone implements, practically flat on both faces, and the sides are nearly but seldom quite parallel. Except in Egyptian examples the blade is generally slightly splayed out; this splay would be a natural result of the hammering necessary to sharpen the edge. Flat celts occur already in predynastic Egypt, prediluvian strata at Susa in Elam and in prehistoric cities on the Indus, as in the earliest metal-using cultures of Cyprus, Crete, the Cyclades and Greece. While most early Oriental specimens are made of copper, the form was reproduced in bronze at Troy and in the Aegean area generally. Simple flat celts are also characteristic of the "Copper Age" in Southern and Eastern Russia, Hungary, Italy, Sardinia, Spain and Ireland. They occur sporadically over a much wider area, even reaching Scandinavia, and are sometimes associated with stone celts (e.g. in the Rhine valley) in hoards and quite often in settlements.

By the beginning of the local Bronze Age the outlines of the flat celt were being modified in Europe. In the British Isles we meet with types whose butts are very narrow in proportion to the wide curving blade (Fig. 3, no. 3). In Bohemia there is a variant with pointed triangular butt, probably an adze-head.

But by this time the typological evolution was already beginning. The first stage in the series is the flanged celt (*Randleistenbeil, hache à rebords élevées*), distinguished by ridges at the sides of either face. These flanges were doubtless in the first instance produced by the hammering on the sides that was in any case necessary after casting in an open mould(5). But they were useful in two ways, both giving the tool increased longitudinal rigidity (diminishing the risk of buckling in the sense of the blow) and preventing the head waggling on its shaft by gripping the prongs of the split branch.

That the value of such flanges was known at least to the ancient Egyptians is shown by a chisel strengthened in this way from the tomb of Hetep-heres, the mother of the Pyramid-builder Cheops (Khufu)(8), but it was apparently never applied to celts in Egypt, Mesopotamia, the Aegean area or even Hungary and Southern Russia. On the other hand, flanged celts, even of copper, occur in Italian tombs, and in bronze they are characteristic of the Early Bronze Age in Italy, Czechoslovakia, Southern Germany, Britain and South-eastern Spain. By a mature phase of that period local variations are observable. Italian specimens always have a nick in the butt formed by leaving intact part of the two jets from the casting in a valve mould (Fig. 4, no. 1); in Bohemian and Central German types the butt is triangular. In the Middle Bronze Age the foregoing types persisted with divergent local variations in certain areas. In Scandinavia, for example, the body is rather long, the sides exactly parallel, and the flanges very

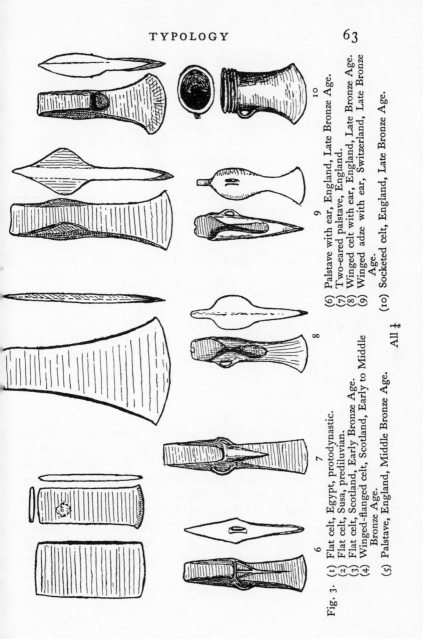

Fig. 3. (1) Flat celt, Egypt, protodynastic.
(2) Flat celt, Susa, prediluvian.
(3) Flat celt, Scotland, Early Bronze Age.
(4) Winged-flanged celt, Scotland, Early to Middle Bronze Age.
(5) Palstave, England, Middle Bronze Age.
(6) Palstave with ear, England, Late Bronze Age.
(7) Two-eared palstave, England.
(8) Winged celt with ear, England, Late Bronze Age.
(9) Winged adze with ear, Switzerland, Late Bronze Age.
(10) Socketed celt, England, Late Bronze Age.

All ¼

prominent (Fig. 4, no. 5). In Western Switzerland and the Rhone valley a type, based on Italian models, grew up distinguished by a great spatuliform blade. At the same time evolutionary improvements were being tried along three distinct lines.

Winged celts (*Lappenbeil, hache à ailerons*)

To diminish further the risk of side-slip a section of the flanges on either face was widened to produce wings that could be hammered round the shaft-prongs on either face. Thus arose the winged celt that was at home in South-west Germany and Upper Italy. At first the wings are in the centre of the implement (Fig. 4, no. 2); towards the close of the Middle Bronze Age they have retreated towards the butt. Then in the Late Bronze Age a loop or ear is added for the thongs that lashed the tool on to its shaft, and the section of the body below the wings is thickened, perhaps under the influence of the palstaves (Fig. 3, no. 8).

Palstaves (*Absatzbeil, hache à talon*)

To prevent the axe-head slipping back up the cleft of the shaft at each stroke and so splitting the knee-stick, a stop-ridge was developed between the flanges to engage the ends of the shaft-prongs. The rudiments of such a stop-ridge are observable on some Early Bronze Age flanged celts both in Great Britain and in Central Europe, but the fully developed palstave belongs to the Middle Bronze Age (Reinecke C) and is character-istic of Scandinavia, North-west Germany, France and Britain (Fig. 3, no. 5). Subsequently the space between the flanges below the stop-ridge was filled up with metal in the casting. A reminiscence of the flanges is for a time preserved in the form of decorative ridges. Especially in Scandinavia one can see very pretty examples of "reminiscent decoration". A tapering ridge is cast on each face of the palstave below the stop-ridge to simulate the prongs of the cleft shaft that had once projected downwards visibly on the faces of the tool. A rather later stage is denoted by the addition of an ear (Fig. 3, no. 6). There is a group of palstaves with two ears, one on each side, in the Iberian Peninsula, Southern France and Sardinia. A few such palstaves have been found in the British Isles (Fig. 3, no. 7), principally in the south and west. These are doubtless imports, but it is generally supposed that the palstave reached the Iberian Peninsula from Britain. It is nevertheless to be noted that implements with two lateral loops and exactly resembling the palstave in plan but flat on both faces are common in Sardinia.

Constricted celts (Böhmisches Absatzbeil)

The advantages of the winged celt and the palstave seem to be combined in a tool called by German archaeologists a Bohemian palstave. It probably grew up as follows. In Switzerland and Bavaria we find a sort of flanged celt that has been hammered so hard on the centre of each side that the body is narrowed while wings develop on either face (Fig. 4, no. 3). The classical Bohemian palstave might result from imitating the product by casting, the section below the wings being again cast solid (Fig. 4, no. 4). This form appears in Bohemia and Moravia during the Middle Bronze Age and was exported to neighbouring territories, particularly Hungary [41].

Socketed celt (*Tullenbeil, hache à douille*)

The natural culmination of all the previous developments was the socketed celt. It no longer requires the splitting of the shaft-end, eliminates side-slip almost entirely and provides a surface to engage the end of the shaft. In the Late Bronze Age this form certainly ousted all its predecessors. According to Montelius it was evolved from one of them, the winged celt. It is supposed that the wings grew till they met round the shaft-prongs, forming a sort of tube divided by a septum (the body of the celt) in the middle. This was then eliminated and the end of the tube closed. It is true that some socketed celts, principally in Italy and Southern Germany where winged celts were current, exhibit semicircular ornaments cast in relief on either side (Fig. 4, no. 7). These certainly imitate wings and, on the theory, are survivals thereof. However, in Hungary and Moravia the socketed celts, instead of the wing pattern, are decorated with ridges forming a V on either face that, just as obviously, reproduce the opening of a constricted celt. And in Scandinavia there are remarkable socketed celts with imitation flanges and a tapering ridge between them on the lower part of the blade (Fig. 4, no. 6). These successfully reproduce the effect of a flanged celt, hafted, and bound round with a bronze collar. Sophus Müller[29] indeed contends that the Danish socketed celt was evolved thus out of the flanged celt with attached bronze collar without the intervention of the winged celt.

None of these *a priori* theories can be accepted. The imitative patterns invoked by Montelius and Sophus Müller were not introduced by the ancient smiths in pious memory of effete devices, but to make a new type of tool look as like as possible the accustomed model of each region, a model with which it was in active competition. Quite possibly the origin of the socketed celt is to be sought outside Europe. There were in Mesopotamia cutting tools, adzes rather than axes, made out of a sheet of metal whose sides were folded round so as to form a tubular socket. Similar implements are known from South Russia, and in the Evans Collection at Oxford is a socketed gouge from Dalmatia formed on this principle.

The centre where European socketed celts were first made has not been exactly determined. The oldest actual examples would be some Danish ones assigned to the Middle Bronze Age. In general the socketed celt belongs to the Late Bronze Age.

T-AXE

The Egyptians, owing probably to the kinds of timber available, did not fix their axe-heads into a split stick but bound them on to a shaft by lashings round and across the head. To facilitate attachment, lugs, continuing the line of the butt, grow out of it on either side by Middle Kingdom times if not before[6] (Fig. 5, no. 1). Stone axe-heads of the same form have been found in Egypt, Central Asia and America.

ADZES

Adzes in general follow the same lines of evolution as the foregoing types of axe-heads. The adze may be narrower and sometimes there is a difference in the slope of one face[6]. Take a cross-section along the length of the implement and draw an imaginary line from the blade to the middle of the butt. Then in an axe the angles made by the two faces with this line must be equal, otherwise each blow will go crooked. In an adze no such symmetry about the major axis is necessary. The real distinction between an axe and an adze is, however, the method of hafting which can seldom be determined from an inspection of the head. Almost any form of celt could be converted into an adze by merely turning the blade through a right angle, e.g. in the case of a knee-shaft by splitting the spur at right angles to the main branch instead of in a line with it. Still in Europe the transverse hafting of the celt to make it do duty as an adze was falling into desuetude in the later part of the Bronze Age. To avoid it the smiths cast palstaves and late winged celts in which the blade was at right angles to the concave faces that received the haft's prongs (Fig. 3, no. 9).

In addition to these simple variants on the axe-head, we should note here one or two peculiar types of celt that generally served as adzes. The proto-dynastic Egyptian adzes and one or two Elamite examples have rounded heads (or butts). Under the Old Kingdom and still more in Middle Kingdom times this rounded head was separated from the body by a marked concave neck (Fig. 5, no. 2).

In the earliest Indian chisels(8) the blade expands slightly till about one-quarter of its length from the butt, then contracts abruptly after a sharp shoulder only to expand again towards the edge. Some adzes of this pattern have been found in Late Minoan Crete and elsewhere in the Eastern Mediterranean region. A flat celt, developed from this type, in which the neck makes a right angle with the shoulders is common in Late Bronze Age hoards in Sicily and Southern Italy. From it grows the trunnion celt or lug-adze where the

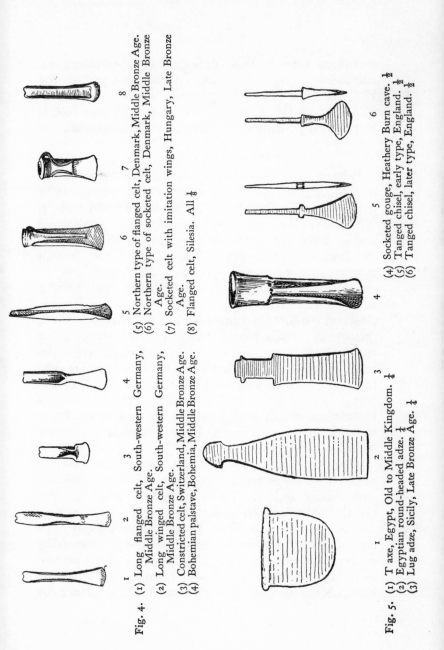

Fig. 4. (1) Long flanged celt, South-western Germany, Middle Bronze Age.
(2) Long winged celt, South-western Germany, Middle Bronze Age.
(3) Constricted celt, Switzerland, Middle Bronze Age.
(4) Bohemian palstave, Bohemia, Middle Bronze Age.
(5) Northern type of flanged celt, Denmark, Middle Bronze Age.
(6) Northern type of socketed celt, Denmark, Middle Bronze Age.
(7) Socketed celt with imitation wings, Hungary, Late Bronze Age.
(8) Flanged celt, Silesia. All ⅛.

Fig. 5. (1) T axe, Egypt, Old to Middle Kingdom. ¼.
(2) Egyptian round-headed adze. ¼.
(3) Lug adze, Sicily, Late Bronze Age. ¼.
(4) Socketed gouge, Heathery Burn cave. ½.
(5) Tanged chisel, early type, England. ½.
(6) Tanged chisel, later type, England. ½.

shoulders have become definite lugs, projecting on either side, a type belonging for the most part to the Hallstatt Iron Age. Its growth, however, interlocks with that of the Sardinian flat celts with two lateral loops already mentioned in discussing palstaves(90).

CHISELS AND GOUGES

Like the adzes, the chisels follow closely the evolution of the celt; the essential feature is the narrowness of the blade. We thus have flat chisels, flanged chisels, flanged chisels with a stop-ridge (very narrow palstaves) and socketed chisels as well as lugged chisels. Late in the Bronze Age of Italy, France and Great Britain tanged chisels appear, probably developed out of shouldered chisels such as we found in most ancient India(5). The earlier variant, found even with palstaves, closely resembles the square-shouldered adze in outline, though the whole tool is naturally more slender, the tang relatively longer and more tapering, while the blade expands very markedly. In the latest Bronze Age the tang is not only narrower but also thinner than the portion below the shoulder; in fact it projects from a flat surface which would engage the end of a tubular wood or bone handle in which the implement must have been held (Fig. 5, no. 6).

Gouges are just chisels with a hollow edge. Implements of this type are known in stone from the Balkans and Russia and in flint from Scandinavia. Copper chisels with a concave blade are known very early in Mesopotamia, from Troy II and from Copper Age graves in South Russia. True socketed gouges, resembling socketed chisels with a concave blade, are very common in the Late Bronze Age all over Europe. But it will be remembered that gouges with the sockets formed by rolling over the metal to form a tube have been found in a Dalmatian hoard. In general it should be noted that socketed chisels and gouges spread more rapidly and earlier than socketed celts (axes). For example, a lake village at Alpenquai near Zurich yielded five socketed chisels and one socketed gouge but no socketed celts; their place was taken by twenty-seven examples of the supposedly older winged type.

AXES (SHAFT-HOLE AXES)

It is curious that the modern type of axe-head that fits on to, not into, the shaft had a very limited distribution down to the later Iron Age. The expedient of providing a hole in the axe-head, parallel to the blade, was indeed known in Mesopotamia in prediluvian times[8]. It was also adopted in Crete and the Aegean islands, in Hungary and Russia at the beginning of the Metal Age in each area and occasionally in Scandinavia, Sicily, Southern Italy, Sardinia and Anatolia. On the other hand, this practical type of metal axe-head was, apart from stray imports, never adopted in Egypt nor yet in any part of Central or Western Europe till late in the Iron Age. Even in Hungary the shaft-hole axe was practically ousted by the socketed celt in the Late Bronze Age.

The shaft-hole axe is apparently a Sumerian invention. Certainly before 3000 B.C. the Sumerians were casting excellent axe-heads with a tube for the shaft reinforced by rings around it and a ridge at the back opposite and parallel to the blade (Fig. 6, no. 1). Of course the manufacture of such an axe required the use of a two-valve mould and a movable core; probably the ridge at the back was originally suggested by the seam, though in practice enlarged to give additional strength at a weak point. Allied types were soon adopted also in Syria. There and in Mesopotamia a curious battle-axe with a very narrow blade was in use during the third and second millennia. The South Russian and Hungarian copper axes for the most part resemble the Sumerian in having a tubular shaft-hole clearly distinguished in profile from the blade (Fig. 6, no. 3). Viewed from above, however, it is seen that the sides of the blade (meeting naturally at the edge) form tangents to the shaft-hole. This peculiarity they share with the early Aegean axes. But such have no tubular extension round the shaft-hole and so look rather like extravagantly thick celts with a perforation joining their sides near the end. The Sicilian and some Russian types conform to the Aegean pattern. The Hungarian axes of the Middle Bronze Age, however, are extraordinarily like mature Mesopotamian types.

TRANSVERSE AXE: SHAFT-HOLE ADZE

Side by side with the weapon described at the beginning of the last paragraph, the inhabitants of the Tigris-Euphrates valleys from the earliest historical periods to the beginning of the Iron Age used an implement identical with the foregoing in respect of its tubular shaft-socket but with the blade turned at right angles to the shaft (Fig. 6, no. 2). This odd type was confined to Babylonia and Assyria with the exception of one specimen from a grave in the Kuban valley north of the Caucasus and one from Syria.

DOUBLE-AXE

The Minoans of Crete preferred an axe with two blades in the same plane and the shaft-hole midway between them. This weapon, which was possibly derived

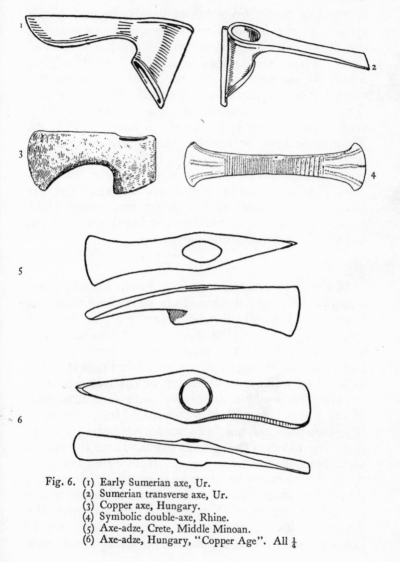

Fig. 6. (1) Early Sumerian axe, Ur.
(2) Sumerian transverse axe, Ur.
(3) Copper axe, Hungary.
(4) Symbolic double-axe, Rhine.
(5) Axe-adze, Crete, Middle Minoan.
(6) Axe-adze, Hungary, "Copper Age". All ¼

in the last resort from Mesopotamia, became a cult symbol in the Minoan religion and was in practical use throughout the Aegean world from Early Minoan times. There are isolated examples from Hungary, South Russia and Sardinia, the latter with a tubular extension of the shaft-hole. In France, Switzerland and Germany a few double-axes of copper are known whose central perforation is too small to take a real shaft. They must then be symbolic and perhaps served as ingots or units of weight (p. 53). In the same connection we may mention an odd implement manufactured in Saxo-Thuringia during the Early Bronze Age. It resembles a double-axe in having two rather blunt blades in the same plane and a shaft-hole between them, but its edges are absurdly narrow[41].

AXE-ADZE

In the Aegean[12] we find from Early Minoan times a tool resembling a double-axe in which one blade has been twisted round till it lies transversely to the shaft and the other blade (Fig. 6, no. 5). A similar type is known from Persia and there is an example from the Kuban which, owing to the character of the shaft-tube, looks exactly like a combination of the two Sumerian axe-types on a single shaft. Axe-adzes are distinctive of the Copper Age of Hungary[41]. Here, it is said, the shaft-hole has not been made by casting but by punching through the red-hot metal. Later the implement reached Sardinia, perhaps from Hungary since the Sardinian examples all have a short tubular projection round the shaft-hole, a feature noticeable on many Hungarian specimens (Fig. 6, no. 6) but strange to the Aegean series. Contemporary with the axe-adzes in Hungary was a sort of axe-hammer that might have been made by breaking off the transverse blade of an axe-adze near the shaft-hole.

BATTLE-AXES

This designation is conventionally restricted to a group of axes with spikes or knobs for the butts that are virtually confined to Hungary and Scandinavia. In Hungary there are two main types: in one the blade expands slightly towards the edge while the butt terminates in a disc. During the Middle Bronze Age this disc is flat or slightly convex; in the Late Bronze Age a large spike projects from it. The other type, confined to the Middle Bronze Age, has a very narrow blade, a long tube for the shaft and a fan-shaped butt. Both types may be richly decorated with engraved scroll patterns. The comparatively rare Danish battle-axes are considerably more massive and generally have a knobbed butt. The majority belong to the Middle Bronze Age and are ornamented with engraved spirals.

DAGGERS

Almost more important for typological chronology than the celts are the daggers, rapiers and swords. The first-named weapons, many of which also served as knives, were current from the beginning of the Metal Age throughout the Old World. The important features in the dagger are the shape of the blade in plan, the provision made against crumpling up under the weight of a thrust (securing longitudinal rigidity) and the attachment of the hilt. The most primitive form of dagger has a roughly triangular blade that is nearly flat on both faces. Triangular daggers are as a rule extremely short, very rarely attaining a length of 6 inches. Any increase in the length must be accompanied by an inconvenient widening of the base if the weapon was not to buckle under the weight of the thrust, unless the increased length were counterbalanced by a thickening of the blade. And, as the dagger was a stabbing weapon, the weight of the blade had to be kept down to preserve the proper balance. A considerable increase of length was, however, possible if the edges were kept parallel for some distance below the hilt before tapering off to a point. This produced the so-called ogival dagger (Fig. 7, no. 7). Both types could be cast in an open mould.

An extension of the blade without undue increase in width, thickness or weight was, however, permitted by casting a thick stout ridge running down the centre— of course in a two-piece mould. This central ridge is termed a midrib and greatly diminished the danger of buckling without affecting the penetrating power (Fig. 7, nos. 4, 5).

All daggers were provided with hilts of wood, horn, ivory or metal. Except in certain Copper Age types the hilts were affixed to the blades by rivets. The hilt, consisting either of a single piece, slitted longitudinally to slip over the blade, or of two pieces, united by nails or lashings, might be attached directly to the butt of the blade or on to a tongue-like projection of the latter, termed a tang. This gives a distinction between tanged and tangless daggers. The tang may be either wiry, in fact a sort of prolongation backwards of the midrib, or flat, but is always narrower than the butt from which it projects like a neck with shoulders on either side. The butt or heel may be either a straight line along the widest part of the blade forming the base of the triangle, or a triangular, trapeze-shaped or semicircular projection of the blade behind that line. When neither rivets nor

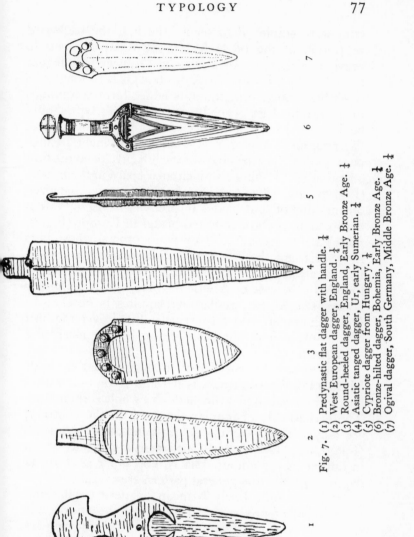

Fig. 7. (1) Predynastic flat dagger with handle. ¼
(2) West European dagger, England. ¼
(3) Round-heeled dagger, England, Early Bronze Age. ¼
(4) Asiatic tanged dagger, Ur, early Sumerian. ¼
(5) Cypriote dagger from Hungary. ½
(6) Bronze-hilted dagger, Bohemia, Early Bronze Age. ¼
(7) Ogival dagger, South Germany, Middle Bronze Age. ¼

tang were employed to secure the hilt, the backward projection of the blade had to be relatively long to prevent waggling. In a curious Copper Age dagger from Western Europe (Fig. 7, no. 2) it is so long as to resemble a tang, but, since its edges form continuous lines from the base of the blade proper, this type should be assigned to the tangless class. In Egyptian tangless daggers, most Aegean types, and all continental European models the broad base of the hilt enveloped the butt on either side leaving a semicircular space in the middle (Fig. 7, nos. 1, 3, 6). This feature is traceable even on the hilts of flint blades in predynastic Egypt. It is conspicuous on bronze-hilted blades in Europe (Fig. 7, no. 6) and is recognizable on many others, whose hilts have perished, by the marks they may have left—a feature always to be looked for as soon as the blade is found. In the case of Asiatic daggers, which are nearly always tanged, no similar overlapping is observable. Often, however, a metal ferrule is fitted over the butt of the blade and the base of the hilt to mask and strengthen the join.

The earliest known Egyptian dagger, dating from Middle Predynastic times, is flat and triangular with a triangular heel, so that the blade as a whole is rhomboid. The earliest Mesopotamian daggers, on the contrary, are tanged and generally strengthened with a midrib (Fig. 7, no. 4). Very early specimens are already ogival in outline. Throughout Asia Minor as far as Troy II daggers of the same general pattern are current.

In Crete some Early Minoan daggers are flat and reminiscent of predynastic Egypt, but the midrib was soon employed, and examples with a broad, flat tang are quite early. The midrib was very pronounced also in Cypriote and Cycladic daggers. In Cyprus a very curious form grew up in which the midrib was prolonged into a long tang bent over at the top (Fig. 7, no. 5). The type, which appeared already in Early Aegean times and lasted till the Late Mycenaean period in the island, was exported to Palestine, Syria, Anatolia and Hungary(18). Weapons, of very similar form but with slits in the blade, as if they had been hafted as spearheads, are known from the Cyclades and Troy II(8).

In Middle Aegean times ogival daggers were in use both in Crete and by the Minyans of Greece. In M.M. I deposits we meet a tanged ogival dagger with slight flanges round the shoulders and bordering the tang. It formed the starting-point for an important series of daggers and rapiers of later Minoan times. The flanges, of course, served to keep in place the plates of wood or ivory that formed the grip of the hilt.

The regular series of continental European daggers begins in the Early Bronze Age with a small flat triangular round-heeled blade, often adorned with groups of grooves parallel to the edges (Fig. 7, no. 3). Before the end of the period such weapons were being provided with hilts of bronze, cast separately, in North Italy, the Rhone valley and Central Europe (Fig. 7, no. 6). In Germany imitations were manufactured with hilts cast in one piece with the blades. From Brittany and England a couple of contemporary daggers have survived whose wooden hilts were studded with hundreds of tiny gold nails.

During the Middle Bronze Age an ogival dagger or short sword was evolved out of the foregoing types in the Rhone valley, preserving their characteristic decoration, rounded heel and flat section. The standard Central European type of this period, however, may have had a different origin, for it has an angular trapeze-

Fig. 8. Rapiers and swords. All ⅛

   (1) Mycenae, Shaft Graves, M.M. III, type I.

   (2) Mycenae, Shaft Graves, M.M. III, type II *a*.

   (3) Mycenae, Shaft Graves, M.M. III, type II *b*.

   (4) Crete, Zafer Papoura, L.M. III, cruciform guards.

   (5) Crete, Zafer Papoura, L.M. III, horned guards.

   (6) South-western Germany, Middle Bronze Age.

   (7) Hungary, Late Bronze Age.

   (8) Bavaria, Middle Bronze Age.

   (9) Hungary, Late Bronze Age.

  (10) Mörigen sword, Switzerland.

  (11) Antennae sword, Switzerland.

  (12) Hallstatt sword of bronze, Early Iron Age, Austria.

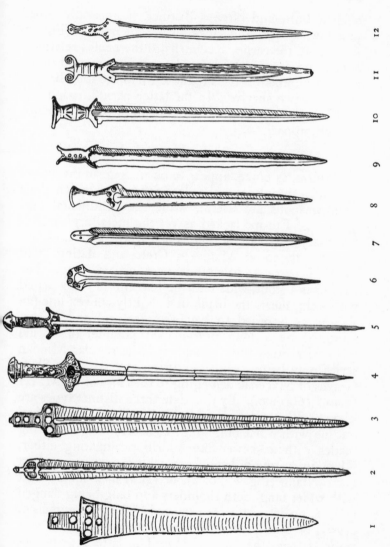

shaped butt, and often a distinct, if generally broad and low, midrib and lacks all ornamentation (Fig. 7, no. 7). In the earlier specimens[43] the heel is relatively broad and carries six rivets; later it is narrowed down and the number of rivets reduced till in the Late Bronze Age only two survive. In the latter period, too, a few specimens with flanged tangs, inspired by Mycenaean models, appear.

RAPIERS

Rapiers, as noted, appear to be an Aegean invention. Orientals shrank from the close fighting in which alone such weapons are useful, while the continental barbarians of Europe lacked as yet the metallurgical skill necessary for their forging. The earliest known rapier, recently found at Mallia in Crete and dating from M.M. I (*circa* 1950 B.C.) is over 90 cm. long. The blade has a stout, wide midrib. The hilt, of ivory plated with gold, meets the blade in a slightly convex line (an Asiatic as opposed to Egyptian feature) and is surmounted by a long pear-shaped pommel of crystal (also very Sumerian looking[13]). The regular Minoan series only begins some centuries later with the Shaft Graves of Mycenae belonging to the close of M.M. III (about 1600 B.C.). By that date three distinct types are known: (I) a relatively flat blade of elongated ogival outline with a flat tang (Fig. 8, no. 1); huge tapering blades with a skewer-like midrib terminating either, (II *a*) in a round heel from which projects a short narrow tang (Fig. 8, no. 2), or (II *b*) in a square butt with wider tang, both shoulders and tang being flanged (Fig. 8, no. 3). All were balanced by heavy pommels of crystal or semi-precious stone to receive which a spur projects from the tang of II *b*. The latter's grip consisted of plates, let in between the hilt's flanges and held in place by large gold-capped rivets. The grip of II *a* was supported by gold mounts fitting over the heel. These already have projections at the shoulder serving as guards to divert from the gripping hand the adversary's weapon when the rapier was parrying a thrust. A short length of the edges, just below the butt, was intentionally blunted so that the thumb and forefinger of the swordsman's hand might rest there—a feature known as the *ricasso*(33).

Later, the flanges on the shoulder of type II *b* were developed into lateral horn-like (L.M. II and L.M. III *a*) or cruciform (L.M. III) projections likewise serving as guards(31) (Fig. 8, no. 4). Late in L.M. III *a*, too, the flange was carried right round the hilt so as to support also the pommel. One or two rapiers of the last-named variety have been found north of the Alps towards the close of the Middle Bronze Age.

The continental European rapiers that begin in the Middle Bronze Age might be regarded as mere prolongations of the ogival dagger. The early specimens have six rivet-holes for the attachment of the hilt (Fig. 8, no. 6). Such weapons, which rarely reach a length of 60 cm., are common in Central Europe and Scandinavia and even reach Great Britain. In the latter country two-piece moulds for their manufacture have actually been found. As in the case of the daggers, the butts of these weapons grew narrower as time went on, yielding in the Late Bronze Age a form with a tapering butt and three rivet-holes, well represented in Southwest Germany, Switzerland and France and occurring sporadically in Hungary and Italy (Fig. 8. no. 7). A contemporary Italian and French variant has a rod-like tang terminating in a hook rather like a Cypriote dagger. The above series was, I believe, inspired by Aegean models. Yet in South-eastern Spain we find, associated with Early Bronze Age celts and daggers, a short flat sword that is clearly just a magnified dagger, preserving the comparatively flat section and round heel of the Early Bronze Age type(2).

Some of the above-mentioned rapier types in Italy, Central Europe and Scandinavia are provided with bronze hilts, cast on, or cast in one piece with, the blade. Early in the Middle Bronze Age (Reinecke B) the hilts are cylindrical or, in South-west Germany, concave (Fig. 8, no. 8). Later in the same period (Reinecke C) a type with octagonal hilt, richly decorated with engraved patterns, arose in the Upper Danube basin. Contemporary Danish sword-hilts are superbly decorated with inlaid spiral patterns. Still later (Reinecke D) the hilts begin to swell out in the middle, but concurrent changes in the shape of the blade indicate that we are now dealing with a new weapon, the cut-and-thrust sword.

SWORDS

All the weapons hitherto described were designed primarily for thrusting. None the less some of the bronze-hilted types from Scandinavia and Central Europe could also be swung. A real sword that can slash as well as thrust must have its centre of gravity shifted towards the blade, while for thrusting the weight had to be in the pommel. Certain long wide blades with a bulge half-way up and a short flat tang, found in Denmark, North Germany, Western Hungary and Upper Italy, seem to be aiming at this result. But a stroke imposes much greater strain on the joint between hilt and blade than does a thrust. The short-tanged type just described could no more grow into a reliable sword than the round- or square-heeled rapier.

True swords seem to begin in a tanged blade whose flat tang and round shoulders are bordered with flanges, as in the Minoan rapiers classed as type II *a*. The form is certainly inspired by rapiers of this family, but the northern and Italian blades in question differ from the Aegean in that the edges are nearly parallel instead of tapering, and the midrib wide and flat so as not to impede a cut (Fig. 8, no. 9). In what Kossinna[38] regards as the earliest type, appearing in Denmark according to Sophus Müller[29] in his period 2, there are no rivet-holes in the tang though there may be four in the heel; lead solder was sometimes used to keep in place the horn plates of the grip. This type occurs principally in Scandinavia, North-eastern Germany and Upper Italy. Some Central European swords with rivet-holes in the tang can hardly be later. They begin in the closing phase of the Middle Bronze Age and flourish in the Late Bronze Age. During the latter phase the blade tends to widen out to a leaf-shape—a barbarous weapon adapted almost exclusively for hacking. In late versions (Reinecke E) nicks are seen just below the shoulder to guard the thumb and forefinger resting on the blunted edge (*ricasso*) above[33]. Others, however, say that the nicks served to prevent the blade joggling out of its scabbard. Sometimes also a spur projects from the end of the tang to hold the pommel. In some West European swords, belonging to a period subsequent to the pure Bronze Age, some of the rivet-holes are replaced by slits. In many of these West European swords the lower end of the blade has been narrowed down, apparently by filing away part of a leaf-shaped blade, with a most curious effect like a carp's tongue.

Early versions of the flange-hilted leaf-shaped sword without any *ricasso* or even marked swelling in the blade are very common in Northern and Central Europe, Styria, Carniola and Bosnia and, as already remarked, even reached Greece and Egypt before 1200 B.C.(32). The immense majority of the late versions, however, come from west of the Rhine, particularly from France and Britain. In the latter country they, with other exotic types, characterize the local Late Bronze Age which is really largely contemporary with the Early Iron Age of Central Europe. There, early in the Hallstatt period, our bronze swords had undergone a further modification, losing altogether the flanges round the hilt and acquiring instead a widened extension thereof to take a conical pommel. This is the true Hallstatt sword, represented by only a few stray examples in Britain (Fig. 8, no. 12).

Parallel to the flange-hilted sword go certain developments of the bronze-hilted rapiers whose blades have been assimilated to the leaf-shaped order. Two important types with a swelling bronze grip of flattened oval cross-section were developed in Switzerland. In one variant, termed the antennae sword (Fig. 8, no. 11), the pommel consists of a stout bronze ribbon bent into opposing spirals. The type is common on both sides of the Alps and is found eastwards as far as Macedonia and Slovakia, northwards into Scandinavia and westwards as far as Lincolnshire. The other Swiss sword, known as the Mörigen or Ronzano type, has a pommel shaped like an oval saucer (Fig. 8, no. 10). Both types begin in the latter half of the Late Bronze Age, Reinecke E, and last into the succeeding phase of the Iron Age. Contemporary with them in Hungary went handsome swords with a swelling grip decorated with raised bands (representing the thongs that bound the plated hilts of the tanged swords) and surmounted with flat or saucer-shaped pommels. Such swords were exported from Hungary to Upper Italy, Eastern France, the Rhine valley and Eastern Galicia.

CHAPES

The rapiers and swords just described were normally carried in wooden sheaths which have naturally perished. We possess, however, some of the bronze chapes in which the scabbards terminated. The Middle Bronze Age chapes resemble little diamond-shaped snuffboxes or end in a loop (Fig. 9, no. 1). The Hallstatt scabbards, on the contrary, ended in weird "winged chapes", a few specimens of which reached Britain (Fig. 9, no. 3). The type more common in Britain and France resembled the last named but was longer and lacked the great lateral wings (Fig. 9, no. 2).

HALBERD (DOLCHSTAB)

The halberd is a peculiar weapon, distinctive of the Early Bronze Age in certain parts of Europe. It is essentially a triangular dagger hafted at right angles to a staff. Indeed a halberd can often be distinguished from a dagger only by observing that the mark left by the haft runs across the blade. Frequently, however, the halberd blade is asymmetrical, i.e. the triangle that would enclose it is scalene and not isosceles (Fig. 9, no. 5).

The weapon is believed to have originated in Southern Spain or Portugal, since certain flint blades found on Copper Age sites there may be best explained as halberds. It is in any case a regular element in the furniture of Early Bronze Age graves along the South-east coast of the peninsula; thence it seems to have reached Upper

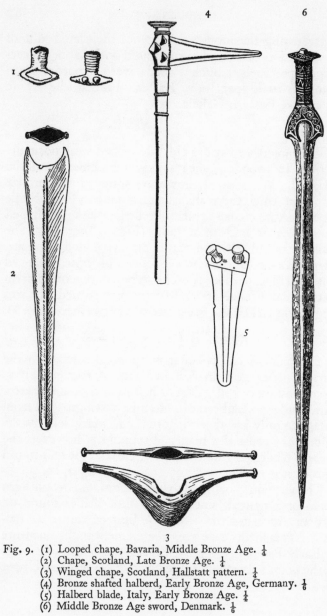

Fig. 9. (1) Looped chape, Bavaria, Middle Bronze Age. ¼
(2) Chape, Scotland, Late Bronze Age. ¼
(3) Winged chape, Scotland, Hallstatt pattern. ¼
(4) Bronze shafted halberd, Early Bronze Age, Germany. ⅛
(5) Halberd blade, Italy, Early Bronze Age. ¼
(6) Middle Bronze Age sword, Denmark. ⅙

Italy, since a few specimens have been found there, and the weapon is depicted, brandished by warriors, on the rocks of the Ligurian Alps. Finally, there is one specimen, markedly asymmetrical and much incurved on the lower edge, from Shaft Grave IV at Mycenae. This halberd, though doubtless inspired by the western group, was a local product since its big rivet-heads have been gilded[12].

Westward from Spain the device was transmitted across the Atlantic to Ireland. A large number of specimens, mostly of copper, are known from the island. Many have a peculiar scythe-like outline. From Ireland a few halberds reached England and Scotland. Thence the type journeyed across the North Sea and up the Elbe where it was adopted in Saxo-Thuringia. Some early halberd blades here are decorated with incised lines like the contemporary daggers. Subsequently a localized variant was created: the haft was sheathed in metal and its head enveloped in a bronze cowl into which the blade was fitted. At first the blade was attached by rivets; in later specimens the cowl has been cast on but shows imitation rivet-heads moulded on its surface (Fig. 9, no. 4). These Central German halberds found their way, presumably by trade, to Sweden, Lithuania and Slovakia. But the weapon was never adopted in Silesia, Czechoslovakia, Hungary, South-western Germany or France.

SPEAR-HEADS

While metal was scarce, missile weapons would naturally be tipped with flint or horn points. At the same time the shorter forms of dagger could easily be converted into lance-heads by attachment to a long shaft. A blade intended specifically for a spear-head, however, would rather have the shape of a laurel or willow leaf. Some sort of tang was usually needed to facilitate union between the blade and the shaft. In Mesopotamia(8), where the shafts (or at least the fore-shafts) were normally made from hollow reeds, the tang was narrow and projected from a marked shoulder at the base of the blade that would engage the outer edge of the reed. The tang in the most popular variant is rectangular in section and tapers off below like a modern poker point. Hence the name "poker-butted spear-head" (Fig. 10, no. 1). The type begins in Sumer before 3000 B.C. and is found also in Elam, North Syria and beyond the Caucasus. In South Russia it persisted throughout the Copper Age into the belated Late Bronze Age (contemporary with the Hallstatt period(105)).

In Egypt a specialized spear-head of metal first appears in early dynastic times(6). The one specimen, known to the author, seems really to conform to the tanged pattern, though it is very rough, but is distinguished by a very broad ferrule of sheet copper that originally encircled both the split end of the shaft and the contained tang. But metal spear-heads are very rare in Egypt till New Kingdom times.

In the Cyclades during the Early Aegean period the shaft of split wood projected a long way down the blade, to which it was attached by thongs. A pair of slits were accordingly left in the blade to receive the bindings(2). From the islands the type spread to Troy II and across the Greek mainland to Levkas(15). Towards the close of Middle Helladic times this slitted spear-head gave birth to an odd form, confined to mainland Greece, in which the tip (or perhaps half the tip) of the shaft fitted into a shoe-like socket cast on one face of the blade. The principal development of the spear-head

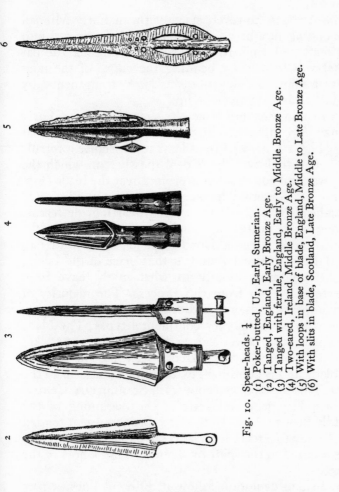

Fig. 10.   Spear-heads. ¼
(1) Poker-butted, Ur, Early Sumerian.
(2) Tanged, England, Early Bronze Age.
(3) Tanged with ferrule, England, Early to Middle Bronze Age.
(4) Two-eared, Ireland, Middle Bronze Age.
(5) With loops in base of blade, England, Middle to Late Bronze Age.
(6) With slits in blade, Scotland, Late Bronze Age.

in the Aegean, however, starts with an Early Minoan type ending in a broad flat tang originally riveted into the shaft. During Middle Minoan times a tubular socket was formed by bending the edges of the tang round a mandril. The tube was later strengthened by forcing a cast ring over its lip.

In Britain there are some kite-shaped blades of Early Bronze Age date terminating in a long, narrow, flat tang (Fig. 10, no. 2). In at least one instance a ferrule had been fitted over the end of the shaft in which the tang was embedded so as to project over the blade (Fig. 10, no. 3). Greenwell has suggested that a true socketed spear-head then developed through casting the ferrule in one piece with the blade and suppressing the tang(34). The Arreton Down type of spear-head (so-called from a hoard found at that place in the Isle of Wight) conforms exactly to what might have been expected to result from this process. The majority of British spear-heads of the Middle Bronze Age, however, agree with contemporary continental types. The blade is shaped like a laurel leaf, and the tube of the socket (formed by core-casting) extends well into the body of the blade and is continued externally as a midrib to the point. This form of head appears in Scandinavia, Central Europe, Hungary and Italy at the beginning of the Middle Bronze Age. In the Late Bronze Age it tended to give way to a form with lanceolate blade. Both types were secured to the shaft by a pin through a hole in the socket.

In Britain evolution followed different lines, a pair of loops developing on the socket through which thongs wrapped round the shaft could pass. These thongs took the place of rivets. In the earlier examples, associated in hoards with the older group of palstaves, and so of

Middle Bronze Age date, the loops stand near the mouth of the socket (Fig. 10, no. 4). This type is purely British, the few examples from North France being certainly imports from across the Channel, though single-eared spear-heads occur in the "Copper Age" of South Russia. Later the loops approach the base of the blade and finally join on to it (Fig. 10, no. 5). Examples even of the last phase are associated with rapiers. In our Late Bronze Age the loops have become either small eyelets near the base of the blade or semicircular slits, generally in the swelling part of a lanceolate blade. The small eyelets may still have had the same functional value as the ancestral loops. They can be paralleled on Sicilian and South Italian spear-heads of bronze belonging there already to the Early Iron Age. The curious semicircular openings (Fig. 10, no. 6), however, can hardly have been designed for receiving binding thongs; there is in fact generally a rivet-hole in the socket of such spear-heads. The type doubtless originated in the British Isles though a derivation from the Early Cycladic slitted form has been suggested by Coffey (57). From Britain specimens were exported as far as Huelva in Spain (92), and the type somehow reached Central and Southern Russia. The idea was adopted and imitated there, moulds for the manufacture of the local variant having been found in the Ukraine (105).

ARROW-HEADS

Metal could only be used for arrow-heads when it was very cheap. Actually flint and bone arrow-heads remained current nearly everywhere throughout the Bronze Age. In Egypt and Crete flint lunates were employed to form transverse heads. In Middle Helladic and Mycenaean tombs we find superb hollow-based (barbed) arrow-heads of flint or obsidian, and cruder variants on the same form are common in the Late Bronze Age urnfields of Central Europe. The finest stemmed and barbed arrow-heads of Britain and France belong exclusively to the Bronze Age. Barbed bone tips are also found in the Late Bronze Age of Italy and Central Europe.

Barbed metal arrow-heads of various patterns but always with a long tapering tang are known from Egypt, Mycenaean Greece and Central Europe during the Middle and Late Bronze Age. In the last-named area the spur-like tang gradually gave way to a tubular socket. The Early Bronze Age graves of South-eastern Spain have yielded a peculiar barbless form with broad leaf-shaped head and a long tail-like tang. It must be remembered that bronze was still used for arrow-heads quite late in the Iron Age.

KNIVES

Many flint knives of the Stone Age had probably been simply backed with wooden handles. Ground stone knives mounted in the same manner are known in Eastern Europe and Asia. A translation of such into metal would be just a strip of copper sharpened along one side by hammering. Such knife-blades with one or two rivet-holes in the back have actually been found in England, France and Central Russia, but generally in a Late Bronze Age context.

Such tools were extremely clumsy, yet it was no easy matter to attach a single-edged knife to a handle so that it should not waggle when pressure was put upon it. Hence single-bladed knives are a late feature. An early group, represented in Old Kingdom Egypt[6] and Troy II[17], solved the problem by prolonging the back

of the blade to form a narrow tapering tang on to which
a tubular handle of wood or bone was fitted (Fig. 11,
no. 1). In Greece such implements do not appear before
Middle Aegean times. Then the hilt was attached by
from three to five rivets (not all in a straight line) to a
wide butt without the use of a tang(3). Later a broad
tang was used to support the handle.

In Central Europe single-edged knives appear first
towards the close of the Middle Bronze Age. All have
arched backs, the handle being either attached by a rivet
to a spur continuing the line of the back (Fig. 11, no. 2)
or cast in one piece with the blade. In the Late Bronze
Age the variety of types is multiplied. The blade is either
straight or recurved. The handle may be of bronze
terminating in a loop and inlaid on either face with
horn plates held in position by a series of metal tabs;
alternatively a wooden handle was fitted into a tubular
socket (Fig. 11, no. 5) or, as in the previous period,
on to a long spur (Fig. 11, no. 6). In Switzerland was
manufactured the curious variant of the latter group,
with a section of solid metal where the ball of the
hand rested, shown in (Fig. 11, no. 7). The type, that
belongs to Reinecke's phase E, was exported as far as
Silesia, Hungary and Central France(41).

In Great Britain single-edged knives are virtually
unknown. But it must be remembered that the short
daggers could be, and doubtless were, used as knives.
They are indeed often termed, very properly, knife-
daggers. In fact some protodynastic Egyptian, Late
Minoan and Early Bronze Age British "daggers" are
rounded off at the point so that their use as daggers is
excluded.

In the British Isles the round-pointed knives of the
Early Bronze Age, that with their round heels and

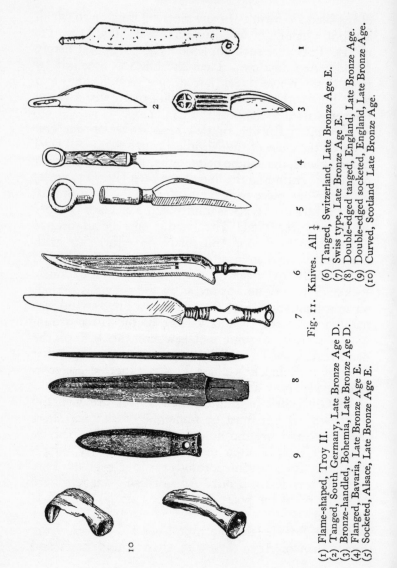

Fig. 11. Knives. All ¼

(1) Flame-shaped, Troy II.
(2) Tanged, South Germany, Late Bronze Age D.
(3) Bronze-handled, Bohemia, Late Bronze Age D.
(4) Flanged, Bavaria, Late Bronze Age E.
(5) Socketed, Alsace, Late Bronze Age E.
(6) Tanged, Switzerland, Late Bronze Age E.
(7) Swiss type, Late Bronze Age E.
(8) Double-edged tanged, England, Late Bronze Age.
(9) Double-edged socketed, England, Late Bronze Age.
(10) Curved, Scotland Late Bronze Age.

numerous rivets are so patently allied to the more pointed "daggers", form the starting-point for two specialized knives of our Late Bronze Age. The first has a long blade and a short flat tang, nearly as wide as the blade, that generally bears two rivets (Fig. 11, no. 8). The second, but that it is found associated with the first, might be regarded as evolved therefrom by the addition of a ferrule like the socketed spear-heads of the Arreton Down class; for it is characterized by an elliptical socket with one or two pairs of rivet-holes, that looks just what might have developed out of such a combination with the hypothetical ferrule (Fig. 11, no. 9). Such forms, though commonest in the British Isles and probably native there, are also found in Northern France and as far south as Charente.

Related to our socketed knives is a curious socketed instrument whose leaf-shaped blade is bent round in a semicircle. Outside Great Britain the type is found in Normandy and perhaps Switzerland (Fig. 11, no. 10).

RAZORS

It is quite possible to shave with a flint blade, and some predynastic flints were undeniably utilized in this way. The early Egyptian metal razors exactly copy these flint forms. One type, confined to the Early Dynastic period, was rectangular with four bevelled edges. Another form, going back to Late Predynastic times, looks like a broad double-edged knife with a short tang. Probably most were sharpened along one edge only as is certainly the case with the specimens from Queen Hetep-heres' tomb. A very similar little implement has recently been found in early Sumerian tombs. The Mesopotamian razors, always unfortunately in bad preservation, are regularly found in pairs; it is uncertain

whether both edges were sharp. In the Aegean area the
earliest certain razors date from the L.M. III period.
The majority are one-edged (Fig. 12, no. 1) but there
are double-edged specimens in which the handle was
riveted directly on to the blade without a tang.

The majority of European razors belong to the same
family. In the earlier graves of the so-called Siculan II
period, containing Mycenaean vases imported from
Greece, we find a long blade with slightly concave sides
and an indentation at the lower end (Fig. 12, no. 3).
The purpose of the indent was perhaps to allow the
forefinger to feel the skin while shaving. In any case
it is a prominent feature in nearly all European double-
edged razors. In contemporary North Italian implements the indent is much more pronounced, and, above,
a wide slit separates the two blades. An openwork
handle, generally terminating in a loop and cast in one
piece with the blade, was attached to these Italian
razors (Fig. 12, no. 5). They belong to the Middle
Bronze Age. Rather later a small group of razors
appears in Franconia and Western Bohemia with a very
broad double-edged blade, sometimes at least divided
by a slit near the end, and an openwork handle cast in
one piece with it (Fig. 12, no. 6). Crude razors of this
pattern are found at a relatively later date in Holland
and Eastern France (Nièvre and Rhône). But the
contemporary Central European razors of phase E have
already grown into developed horseshoe-shaped blades
(Fig. 12, no. 7).

In Upper Italy, on the other hand, during the Late
Bronze Age and first phase of the Early Iron Age
(Villanova culture), the razor assumes a rectangular
outline, preserving the indent in the lower end as an
almost circular aperture and provided with a loop of

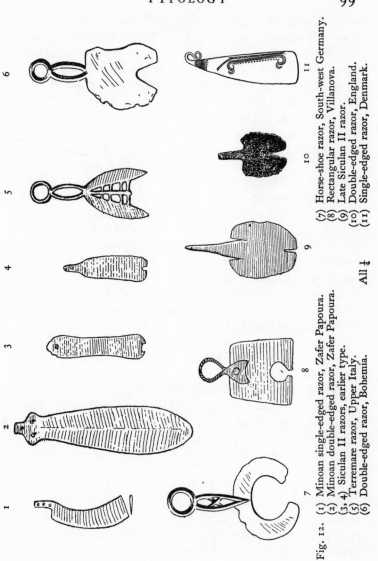

Fig. 12. (1) Minoan single-edged razor, Zafer Papoura.
(2) Minoan double-edged razor, Zafer Papoura.
(3, 4) Siculan II razors, earlier type.
(5) Terremare razor, Upper Italy.
(6) Double-edged razor, Bohemia.
(7) Horse-shoe razor, South-west Germany.
(8) Rectangular razor, Villanova.
(9) Late Siculan II razor.
(10) Double-edged razor, England.
(11) Single-edged razor, Denmark.

All ¼

twisted wire riveted on to the blade as handle (Fig. 12, no. 8). The same type is found in South Italy and Sicily, but in that island a type, derived from the earlier native form, but with wider blade, more pronounced slit between the edges and a flat tang for handle, is also encountered in the later tombs of the Siculan II period. Similar forms occur in Southern France (Ariège and Charente) and probably give a clue to the ancestry of our British razors (35).

The latter resemble a maple leaf in form. A tang to take the handle projects from the base of the blade and is often continued downwards by a wide midrib along its face. In the opposite end is a deep V-shaped indent and just behind it a circular eyelet. Though generally Late Bronze Age in date, one such blade, though without the round eyelet, was found with rapiers and palstaves in Scotland (60). It is generally believed that these razors belong to the group of foreign forms introduced into Britain by invaders arriving at the beginning of the Late Bronze Age. The affinities of our razors in any case seem to lie rather with Sicily and the Western Mediterranean than with the countries east of the Rhine.

While the standard European razors of the Bronze Age were double-edged, there is a series in Scandinavia with only one blade. Such are doubtless in the last resort derived from the normal Mycenaean implement (Fig. 12, no. 11, cf. 1).

TWEEZERS

Another surer but certainly more painful method of removing the facial hairs was to pull them out with tweezers. Depilatory tweezers, formed essentially of a bronze ribbon bent double and rather wider at the ends than at the middle, were largely used in predynastic Egypt and precede razors in Crete and the Cyclades, appearing there in Early Aegean times. In Central Europe and Scandinavia, tweezers, allied to the fore-going, were adopted in the Middle Bronze Age, slightly preceding the razors, though curiously enough razors and tweezers are not seldom found together in the same grave. Such metal tweezers are very rare in Britain but appear at the same time as the razors in the Late Bronze Age.

A different type of tweezer, consisting of two strips of metal brazed together, was current in Mesopotamia and India about 3000 B.C. They are found as components of toilet-sets, hung on a ring together with a pricking instrument and an ear-scoop(8). As their ends are very narrow, these Asiatic tweezers probably served a different purpose to the Egyptian, perhaps catching lice. Structurally, a curious pair of bone tweezers from an Early Bronze Age grave in England resembles the Asiatic group.

SICKLES

All metal sickles go back in the last resort to the so-called jaw-bone sickle formed by inserting serrated flint blades into the dental cavity of some domestic animal. No jaw-bones thus equipped have ever been found, but Egypt has yielded a wooden mount, armed with flints, shaped in imitation of a jaw-bone, and similarly formed clay sickles are common in prediluvian deposits in Mesopotamia. As a result of this origin a hollow arc-shaped cutting edge is universal in the metal sickles, but three main groups can be distinguished by the method of hafting the blade.

In the oldest Mesopotamian metal sickle the blade

was continued into a flat tang which was doubled over to form a loop. The same type is found in Anatolia in Troy VI, and a variant appears in the Late Bronze Age of the Caucasus and Transylvania.

In the commonest North European type, found also in Southern Germany, Bohemia, Eastern France and England, there is no tang. The blade is reinforced by a couple of ridges parallel to it on the back, and the handle is attached with the aid of a knob projecting on one face near the butt. It is therefore termed the button sickle (Fig. 13, no. 1). This type certainly goes back to the Middle Bronze Age.

During the Late Bronze Age it was replaced in France and Central Europe by a type of Italian or Hungarian origin. In the latter the form of the blade is the same, but the button is replaced by a wide tang that makes an angle with the blade. The handle was attached by a rivet and is kept in place by a pair of ridges running along the edges of the tang (Fig. 13, no. 2).

The socketed sickle may have been evolved out of the foregoing, since its tubular socket makes a similar angle with the blade. The type was certainly invented in the British Isles where it is common in hoards of the Late Bronze Age (Fig. 13, no. 3). Stray specimens, presumably British exports, occur beyond the Channel in Northern France, the Swiss lake-dwellings and Upper Italy. The device even reached Sardinia where a local variant on it occurs.

HARNESS

The harnessing of animal motive power was, as already remarked, one of the most momentous achievements of the Bronze Age. Yet of all the gear that must have been used in the application of that new motive

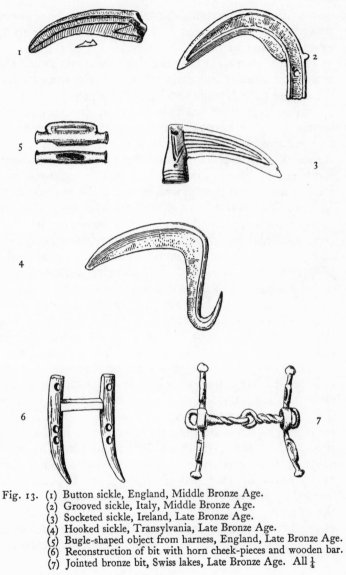

Fig. 13. (1) Button sickle, England, Middle Bronze Age.
(2) Grooved sickle, Italy, Middle Bronze Age.
(3) Socketed sickle, Ireland, Late Bronze Age.
(4) Hooked sickle, Transylvania, Late Bronze Age.
(5) Bugle-shaped object from harness, England, Late Bronze Age.
(6) Reconstruction of bit with horn cheek-pieces and wooden bar.
(7) Jointed bronze bit, Swiss lakes, Late Bronze Age. All ¼

power the only recognizable elements that have come
down to us from Bronze Age Europe are bits, or to be
exact, portions of bits.

It is still uncertain how the Sumerians controlled the
asses that drew their early chariots. Even as late as
the Eighteenth Dynasty in Egypt it is possible that the
chariot horses were governed merely by nose-ropes;
for though several royal tombs have yielded us chariots
and harness, no bits have as yet come to light. The
earliest known metal bit comes from a Late Mycenaean
tomb at Mycenae. Like modern bits, it consisted of a
jointed metal rod that passed between the horse's jaws.
But in addition it was equipped at either end with flat
pieces of metal, termed cheek-pieces, to which the reins
were attached by loops. When the reins were drawn
tight the cheek-pieces would compress the animal's
jaws, the pain in the case before us being augmented by
metal spikes on the inner faces of the cheek-pieces[6].

No such metal bits are known during the pure
Bronze Age of continental Europe. But from the
"terremare" of Upper Italy and Middle Bronze Age
deposits in Hungary, Germany and Sweden we possess
pieces of tine or horn with several perforations that are
believed to have been attached as cheek-pieces to the
ends of a bar of wood or a stout twisted strip of hide
that constituted the bit proper (Fig. 13, no. 6). Similar
horn cheek-pieces become quite common in the Late
Bronze Age and even reach Britain in company with
other continental types. But in Switzerland and
Scandinavia by that phase of the Late Bronze Age,
termed by Reinecke Hallstatt A (Bronze Age E), and in
the contemporary Early Iron Age deposits of Upper
Italy, bronze bits were being already manufactured.
These all have metal cheek-pieces, generally bent rods

with loops at the sides or slits through them to take
the reins (Fig. 13, no. 7).   Only later in the Hallstatt
period do we meet examples of the modern form of bit
terminating in rings.

ORNAMENTS

The ornaments worn during the Bronze Age are far
too varied to be discussed in detail. They are, moreover,
specialized into local groups that can best be mentioned
later in dealing with the several cultures.   Some, however, throw an unique light on cultural relations or
serve as invaluable chronological guides.   Such must
be briefly described here.

PINS

Pins were used for fastening garments over a curiously
restricted area during the earlier parts of the Bronze
Age. Their use must obviously be correlated with a
particular costume—an untailored cloak or mantle,
worn over the shoulders and fastened in front by one
or two pins. As a matter of fact ancient representations
or lucky finds in peat-bogs afford positive proof of the
wearing of such a garb among the Sumerians and the
prehistoric Danes. Pins, and the dress they imply,
were worn in Mesopotamia from the earliest Sumerian
times and then throughout Asia Minor and Anatolia.
They were also freely used in the Cyclades and on the
Greek mainland during Early Aegean times, but only
very rarely and in an immature form in Crete. Pins
are equally rare in centres of metallurgy connected with
maritime trade westward—Sicily, Sardinia, Spain and
Britain. On the other hand they were adopted together
with metallurgy in Central Europe, whence the local
types spread widely as a result of ethnic movements.

To keep the pin in position a thread was passed
through or tied on to its head, looped round the fold of
the stuff to be fastened, and the end wound round the
shaft again. The devices employed for attaching the
thread provide the most workable basis for a classifica-
tion of pins.

(I) PINS WITH LOOPED HEADS

In this class the head itself is a loop through which
the thread may be passed. The simplest way of making
such a pin is to take a piece of wire and bend over
the top end or head. Generally the head is hammered
out flat before being bent over.[1] The result is termed
a roll-head pin (*Rollennadel*) (Fig. 14, no. 1). Such
are found from the earliest times in Sumer and throughout the Asiatic Bronze Age province and its Central and
North European extensions. A natural development of
this is the shepherd's-crook pin distinctive of the Bronze
Age in East Central Europe. A roll-head pin might be
made more ornate by simply widening the flat head.
From merely broadening the head materially in this way
arises the racket pin (*Rudernadel*). This variant is found
in Sumer before 3000 B.C. (Fig. 14, no. 3), then in the
Early and Middle Bronze Ages of Hungary and Central
Europe and later in the Caucasus. In the Early Bronze
Age of Central Europe the decorative effect was further
enhanced by trimming off the angles of the flat plate
till it became a perfect circle (a little tang being left
projecting opposite the shaft to form the loop), the
disk pin (*Scheibennadel*). The disk is often decorated
with an engraved cross. By casting the disk as an

[1] At first this flat head may just have been part of the original ribbon
from which the wire was manufactured by the torsion process described
on p. 37.

openwork wheel with an ear to represent the original folded loop, the wheel pin was created in the Rhine valley during the Middle Bronze Age (Fig. 14, no. 4). The type was exported throughout Central Europe as far as Upper Italy, Poland and Denmark.

An earlier variant of the disk pin, also formed by trimming up a racket pin, was the trefoil pin of the Rhône valley. The bilobate and trilobate pins of the Middle Bronze Age in Upper Italy may be derived from it in the same way as the wheel pin from the disk type.

A safer loop might be produced on a wire pin by bending the top over and twisting it round the shaft, producing the knot-headed pin (*Schleifennadel*). The principle was known both in predynastic Egypt, in early Sumer and in prehistoric cities on the Indus. It was applied to the manufacture of pins in Cyprus and Troy II. Thence the type was diffused up the Danube to Hungary, Bohemia and Silesia, where it became common from the beginning of the age of metals and throughout the Middle Bronze Age (Fig. 14, no. 5). By imitating the knot-headed pin in a casting the Aunjetitz pin (*Böhmische Osennadel*) was created in Bohemia. It had an inverted conical head surmounted by a cast loop or ear (Fig. 14, no. 6). The ring-headed pin seems a later derivative of the same fundamental type.

(2) TOGGLE OR EYELET PINS

In a second series the thread was passed through a hole in the pin-shaft near its head. The shaft had generally to be widened where it was pierced. In Mesopotamia by 3000 B.C. it was hammered out flat, and the flattened surface perforated (Fig. 14, no. 2). The wide flat part, often called the neck, is frequently

Fig. 14. (1) Roll-headed pin, Kish, Early Sumerian.

(2) Toggle pin, Kish, Early Sumerian.

(3) Racket pin, Ur, Early Sumerian.

(4) Wheel pin, South-west Germany, Middle Bronze Age.

(5) Knot-headed pin, Bohemia, Early Bronze Age.

(6) Aunjetitz pin, Bohemia, Early Bronze Age.

(7) Pin with bent disk head, Bohemia, Late Bronze Age.

(8) Sunflower pin, Ireland, Late Bronze Age.

(9) Pin with lateral loop, England, Late Bronze Age.

(10) Ribbed pin, Alsace, Late Bronze Age.

(11) Vase-headed pin, Bavaria, Late Bronze Age.

(12) Violin-bow fibula, Switzerland, Middle Bronze Age.

(13) Simple arc fibula, Italy, Late Bronze Age.

(14) Hungarian fibula with looped bow, Late Bronze Age.

(15) Elbow fibula, Siculan II.

(16) Two-piece fibula, Denmark, Middle Bronze Age.

(17) Two-piece fibula, Denmark, Late Bronze Age.

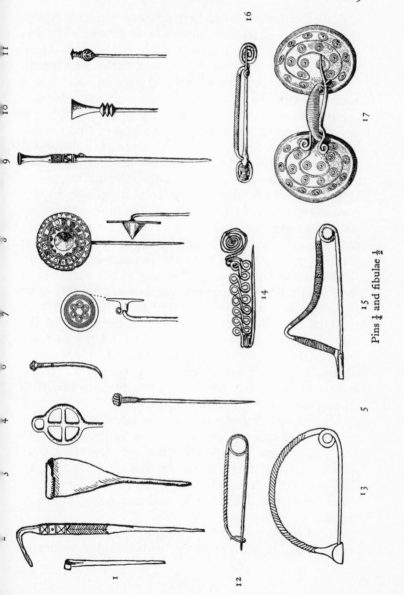

Pins ¼ and fibulae ½

engraved with crosses and herring-bone patterns. Above the neck the shaft was normally bent over. It was generally surmounted with a globular bead of lapis. Eyelet pins with bulbous, or in Cyprus mushroom, heads, cast in one piece with the shaft, very early found acceptance in Syria, Cyprus, Troy and South Russia. Eyelet pins did not reach Central Europe till the Middle Bronze Age, but are very characteristic of that period. The round swollen necks of these pins are decorated with just the same herring-bone and cruciform patterns as the Sumerian pins of the fourth millennium.

In South Germany the eyelet pins seldom have a specialized head. In Hungary, on the other hand, they are surmounted with mushroom heads. In some mushroom pins the eyelet is formed by a spur projecting from the side of the shaft to meet the (separately cast) head. Allied to these is a form belonging to the very end of the Middle Bronze Age: the flat disk head is cast apart from the shaft and with a socket fitted on to the bent shaft so that the latter is parallel to the plane of the disk. The eye is formed by a looped strand of finer wire, one end of which was cast on to the shaft, the other tucked into the head's socket (Fig. 14, no. 7). In its Bohemian home the disk was generally decorated with an engraved star pattern. A variant with no loop or eyelet reached Scandinavia in the latest Bronze Age there (Montelius IV and V) and Great Britain. These late pins, termed sunflower pins, are decorated only with concentric circles upon the disk (Fig. 14, no. 8). The sunflower pin is the only type at any time at all common in the British Isles till our own Iron Age began.

Allied to the pins with perforated neck is a rare type with a lateral loop on the neck. It is found occasionally in Early Bronze Age graves in North Syria. Then there are isolated examples from Bohemia belonging to the very end of the Middle Bronze Age, from Denmark later still, from the great Iron Age cemetery at Hallstatt in Upper Austria and from France undated. Yet the type has been found in Scotland in company with Middle Bronze Age rapiers and palstaves and a razor (Fig. 14, no. 9).

Carefully to be distinguished from the foregoing is the "East German eyelet pin" found in the Late Bronze Age urnfields. Its distinctive feature is a lateral spur on the neck perforated with a hole *parallel to the shaft*. It is probably derived from a pin common in Hungary and Central Europe in the Early and Middle Bronze Ages with a bulbous head perforated with a hole running down from the crown to the side of the shaft. This type may be inspired by Syrian bulb-headed pins.

(3) PINS WITH MERELY DECORATIVE HEADS

In a third family of pins the securing thread was merely twisted round the head; the latter, therefore, need not be perforated but is generally decorative. From ancient Sumerian and Early Cycladic graves come pins with animal heads, while others from Troy II were surmounted by miniature vases. In an important group extending from Turkestan to Italy the head is just a spiral disk. In some Early Cycladic specimens two spirals sprout out from the top of the shaft, and the same happens in Italy during the Middle Bronze Age and then in Central Europe, where spiral-headed pins are late in the Late Bronze Age.

Indeed, throughout continental Europe loops and eyelets went out of fashion during the Late Bronze Age.

The older eyelet pins are replaced by forms, often of gigantic size, with a collar of ribs or a big head in the shape of a vase, a poppy-head, a turban or a globe. Very distinctive of the second phase of the Late Bronze Age (Kraft E) are the Swiss pins whose globular heads are adorned with inlaid "eyes". Later, fashions changed again; the giant types disappear, and the heads of the rest shrink.

SAFETY-PINS OR FIBULAE

A logical corrolary of the pins kept in position by a loop of thread round the fold of clothing pierced by the pin was the safety-pin or brooch, technically known by the Latin name of *fibula*. There are two methods by which a safety-pin might be arrived at. You might take a wiry pin and bend back the top of the shaft over the fold of clothing to meet the lower part of the shaft and catch the point. Alternatively the thread passing through the eyelet of a toggle pin might be replaced by a length of wire which would likewise be twisted so as to catch the point. The first plan produces our safety-pin or one-piece fibula; the alternative gives rise to the so-called two-membered safety-pin. These two series seem to be independent, but both start about the same time, Middle Bronze Age or *circa* 1350 B.C., and moreover at opposite ends of the amber trade route. The one-piece safety-pin originated in Italy, Bohemia, or, on the latest theory, Mycenaean Greece; the two-membered fibula started about the same time in Denmark. It is therefore on the face of it unlikely that the two types are really autonomous and spontaneous growths.

ONE PIECE SAFETY-PINS.

In Late Minoan Crete people wore long pins, with a twisted shaft but no distinct head, whose upper parts were just hooked over. Blinkenberg(36) and Myres(37) believe that these pins were turned into fibulae by the simple expedient of bending the upper end into a hook to catch and also guard the point. This terminal hook is thus the prototype of the catch-plate. To make a really workable safety-pin the simple hooked end had to be modified so as to give a protection to the point, and a spring had to be introduced to bring the point back into the catch. The fibulae from pure L.M. III *a* tombs in Greece have a bow parallel to the pin and a catch-plate formed either by hammering out the end of the wire flat or by coiling it in a spiral (Fig. 14, no. 12). Such fibulae are known as the violin-bow type and form the starting-point for several series, developing along divergent lines in different regions. The greater part of this evolution lies outside the scope of this book, in the Iron Age, but some early forms may be sketched here.

Violin-bow fibulae, representing the primary stage of the safety-pin, are found outside Greece in Middle Bronze Age deposits in Italy and Sicily, and rather later in Bosnia, the Tyrol and Switzerland. There are two specimens from Central Europe, alleged to come from Early Bronze Age graves, but the circumstances of their discovery are doubtful.

The changes affect principally the form of the bow, aiming at making it more ornate or capable of catching a thicker fold of clothing. In Greece during the Mycenaean period the bow was widened to a leaf-shape. Rather later a series of figure-8 twists were introduced

in the wire bow. The latter type occurs on both sides
of the Adriatic and in North-western Hungary (Fig. 14,
no. 14). In the last-named region it gave rise to a series
of highly elaborate variants in the Late Bronze Age and
Hallstatt period.

The main direction of evolution went towards increasing the space between pin and bow to allow of
more stuff being gripped. This was effected by four
methods, giving rise to four main families that constitute the second evolutionary phase: A 1, prolonging
the catch-plate vertically, giving the asymmetrical bow
fibula; A 2, bending the bow into a semicircle, producing
the arc fibula; A 3, twisting the bow up into an elbow
and elongating the stilt, yielding the elbow and serpentine fibulae, or A 4, adding coils to the spring, leading
to the harp fibula. Of these only the last version
preserves the spiral catch-plate. The first two, on the
other hand, as well as some late violin-bow types, may
have small shoulders or beads at either end of the bow.

The arc fibula (Fig. 14, no. 13) appears in Greece
already during L.M. III *b* times and in the Late Bronze
Age of Italy and Bosnia, and leads to many variants in
the Iron Age. The elbow fibula (*a gomito*) (Fig. 14,
no. 15) is found in Sicily in graves of the Siculan II
period slightly later than those containing Mycenaean
vases. In the Early Iron Age of Cyprus a kindred form
is found. A rather later Sicilian type (*serpeggianti ad
occhio*) introduces a second loop at the root of the stilt
where the elbow comes. It seems influenced by a
version of the arc fibula, with a loop at the base of the
catch-plate, found during the Early Iron Age in Crete
and Illyria. Finally the harp fibula, appearing in a
rudimentary form in the latest Bronze Age of Styria,
characterizes the early Hallstatt period in the Eastern

Alps and Lower Austria. Contemporary with it in Styria appears the earliest spectacle brooch, a type distinctive of the true Hallstatt culture and of the Geometric period in Greece. It consists of a strand of wire coiled into a pair of spiral disks; from the centre of one the wire, sharpened to make the pin, is brought back across the other to engage in its end.

The modifications introduced during phase III of the safety-pin's evolution include, in the case of arc fibulae, threading beads on to the bow or imitating such in metal bulbs cast on it (Greece and Italy), widening the catch-plate (Greece and Illyria) or lengthening it (Italy), introducing a second loop at the root of the catch-plate (Greece and Illyria, also Sicily), decorating the bows with raised ribs (Upper Italy and Switzerland), etc.

These three stages can be approximately dated. Stage I is purely Mycenaean and accordingly begins before 1300 B.C.; even stage II began before the end of the Mycenaean age, about 1100; while stage III was already well advanced in sub-Mycenaean times by 1000 B.C.

TWO-MEMBER FIBULAE

The evolution of the two-piece fibulae follows in the main the same lines as that of the one-member group. During the first or Middle Bronze Age phase (Sophus Müller, 3) the bow, either of twisted wire or leaf-shaped, is parallel to the pin and ends in two spiral disks or just two hooks. The pin is just a normal toggle pin with swollen, perforated neck and simple, club-shaped head (Fig. 14, no. 16). This stage is virtually confined to Denmark. During the Late Bronze Age divergent developments set in as the device spread. In Scandinavia and North Germany the pin acquires a double-T-shaped head; in Central Germany the bow is widened out to an oval or rhombic plate, often beautifully decorated with engraved lines. Then the bow is arched into an arc, as farther south, and at the same time (Montelius IV, Reinecke Hallstatt A) the spiral disks of wire are replaced by cast plates that may be adorned with patterns cast in relief or engraved (Fig. 14, no. 17).

In conclusion a word may be said on the distribution of safety-pins in barbarian Europe. About 1300 B.C. they were being worn generally only in Upper Italy (omitting Greece and Sicily) on the one hand and in Denmark on the other. Then their use spread from these two centres, but mainly to the east of the central amber route. From Denmark two-piece fibulae spread all over North Germany to Silesia, and a few crossed the Sudeten Mountains and reached the Upper Danube and the Upper Rhine. About the same time one-piece brooches were coming into fashion in the North Balkans, and eastward from the Alps to Slovakia, while an advance guard was appearing in the Tyrol and Switzerland. Curiously enough simple arc fibulae were also adopted in the Caucasus. But in the whole of Western Europe, the Hungarian plain and Russia the device had not been adopted before the end of the local Bronze Ages. Even in Central Europe the spread of the two-member fibula from the North was arrested by the advance of the Hallstatt culture. With the latter one-piece safety-pins were carried eastward across the Hungarian plain into Transylvania, up the March into East Germany, across Bavaria into the Rhine valley and thence or through Switzerland over France.

BRACELETS, ANKLETS AND COLLARS

It is to-day regarded as a sign of barbarism to load the person with heavy metal ornaments. And so too among the civilized peoples of the Ancient East and the Aegean, metal bangles and similar trappings are rare. The contemporary barbarians of Europe, on the contrary, loved to deck their necks, wrists, arms and legs with open rings or coiled cylinders of bronze.

The great majority of ornaments of this class, apart from cylinders, are penannular; they do not, that is, form closed rings. The simplest form is just an open ring of metal produced by casting or bending a rod. Cross-section and thickness vary considerably. In the Early Bronze Age the ends generally taper off but without reaching a point. In the Middle Bronze Age, after narrowing down slightly from the centre of the arc, the ends of the heavier forms are thickened or expanded, forming what the Germans call *Endstollen*. An exaggeration of such thickening leads to the cup-shaped ends fashionable during the Late Bronze Age in the British Isles. During the Middle Bronze Age of Hungary and Central Europe the heavier bracelets, smooth inside and convex without, were tastefully decorated with engraved and punctured arcs and triangles. In the Late Bronze Age especially in Bavaria and Switzerland the engraved decoration was replaced by cast ribs as in the case of contemporary pins (Fig. 15, no. 1). The massive forms might be replaced by cheaper and lighter substitutes made out of stout ribbon, hollow or flat on the inner side. Out of these grow huge hollow or tubular armlets, cast by the *cire perdue* process on a core and decorated with concentric circles and semicircles joined up by parallel lines, that were a

Fig. 15. (1) Heavy ribbed armlet, Bavaria, Late Bronze Age. $\frac{1}{4}$

(2) Gold armlet, Ireland, Middle to Late Bronze Age. $\frac{1}{4}$

(3) Hungarian armlet, with spiral ends, Middle Bronze Age. $\frac{1}{4}$

(4) Horizontally ribbed armlet, Hungary, Middle Bronze Age. $\frac{1}{4}$

(5) Hooked double armlet, England, Middle Bronze Age. $\frac{1}{4}$

(6) Spiral-ended anklet, Alsace, Late Bronze Age. $\frac{1}{4}$

(7) Ingot torque, Bohemia, Early Bronze Age. $\frac{1}{4}$

(8) Gold ear-ring, Troy II. $\frac{1}{2}$

(9) Twisted gold armlet, England. $\frac{1}{4}$

(10) Spiral-ended finger-ring, South Germany. $\frac{1}{3}$

(11) Helical wire tutulus, Bavaria, Early Bronze Age. $\frac{1}{4}$

(12) Spiked tutulus, Hungary, Middle Bronze Age. $\frac{1}{4}$

(13, 14) Gold lock-rings, Early and Middle Bronze Age. $\frac{1}{2}$

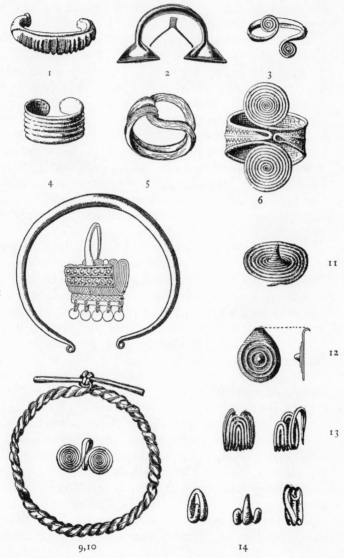

speciality of the Swiss lake-dwellings during the last phase of the Bronze Age (Kraft E).

Bracelets with spiral ends were characteristic of East Central Europe, Hungary, Galicia, East Germany and Scandinavia during the Middle and Late Bronze Age. The most handsome Middle Bronze Age type in the former area terminates in opposed spiral disks. Such rings were worn on the upper arm as the traces of wear indicate. Later Hungarian specimens, belonging already to phase E of the Bronze Age, have double-spiral ends. A variant, also with double-spiral ends but a ribbon-like body decorated with cast horizontal ribs or engraved triangles, is, however, found already in Middle Bronze Age deposits of Scandinavia, South-west Germany and Bohemia.

Two types of bracelet formed from a doubled piece of wire deserve notice. In the variety current in Central Europe from Early Bronze Age times the ends of the wire are twisted; in a British type of the Middle Bronze Age, the loop where the wire is bent back is relatively wide and the ends are twisted over and hooked into it (Fig. 15, no. 5). Neither type is penannular; both approximate rather to the cylinders.

Broad armlets of plate bronze, even in width all over and decorated with cast horizontal ribs or engraved triangles, appear already in the Early Bronze Age of Central Europe. Analogous types, generally narrower and with sharper ridges, are found in contemporary deposits in France and Britain. Such wide armlets may have taken the place of the stone wrist-guards worn by the archers of the Bell-beaker culture in the Copper Age to protect them from the recoil of the bow-string. The horizontally ribbed armlet persists into the Late Bronze Age, even reaching Scandinavia. But the later Central

European specimens generally have rounded ends (Fig. 15, no. 4).

East of the Rhine the tendency was to replace broad armlets by cylinders. Cylinders of narrow copper ribbon had been worn even in the Copper Age and, made of stouter ribbon, appear in Early Bronze Age hoards. By the Middle Bronze Age they had become very popular, particularly in East Germany and Hungary. Here the ribbon, hammered out to nearly an inch or so in width, is decorated with punctured patterns and strengthened with a midrib which is prolonged beyond either end of the ribbon and coiled into spiral disks. The type outlasts the Bronze Age and reappears in Early Iron Age graves in Italy and the Caucasus. Cylinders of the same structure could be worn on the legs.

A series of anklets, developed in the Upper Rhine valley, is interesting owing to its well-marked typological evolution. The oldest form, going back to Reinecke's phase B, is a simple piece of stout wire coiled into spiral disks at either end. Next, the wire body is replaced by narrow ribbon, the spiral ends remaining wiry. Finally in phases D and E the ribbon of the body is widened and the wiry ends are bent back and carried round for one turn before being coiled into spirals (Fig. 15, no. 6). This late type reaches the Upper Danube on the one hand and the French Departments of Aube, Marne and Côte d'Or on the other.

There remains a series of ornaments with wiry bodies, worn principally on the neck, which are of special importance owing to early parallels on the fringes of the Oriental civilizations. A penannular ring of stout wire with the ends hammered flat and bent back into loops (Fig. 16, no. 7) is represented by a number of specimens in a hoard found at Byblos in North Syria and dated roughly about 1800 B.C. There are stray specimens from Egypt of a similar age, and later the type was common in the Caucasus. Just the same rings are found in the very earliest Bronze Age deposits of Hungary and Central Europe. Here they were sometimes worn as collars and also, as noted on p. 30, used as ingots. They are therefore termed ingot torques. From Central Europe the type reached the valleys of the Rhine and Rhône. Ingot torques remained current throughout the Bronze Age, but some of the later specimens are made of twisted rectangular wire,[1] a feature also observed on certain early Syrian specimens. The effect of torsion was imitated in casting on some European examples.

A series of ingot torques diminishing in size might be fastened together by pins through the terminal loops to form gorgets. Composite gorgets of this pattern are actually found as late as phase E in South-west Germany. But imitations thereof in sheet bronze with the ends rolled up into tubes were current in Switzerland and Scandinavia during the Middle Bronze Age. The Swiss collars are decorated with engraved rectilinear patterns and maintain the same width throughout their circumference. The Scandinavian, on the other hand, are shaped so as to be widest in the middle. The earlier ones show horizontal ribs in front, reminiscent of the originally separate neck-rings, but panels at either end are richly ornamented with engraved spirals. Related to the foregoing are some collars of thin sheet gold from Brittany and Portugal. Instead of ribs, these exhibit in

---

[1] The name *torque*, derived from the Latin *torqueo*, I twist, should strictly be applied only to such twisted rings, but is in practice used for all neck-rings whether smooth or twisted.

front, slits, reproducing the effect of the originally separate rings.

A hoard found in the ruins of Troy II included a gold collar or bracelet of twisted rectangular wire with hooked ends, and a similar torque of silver wire has come to light in an Early Helladic grave on Levkas. Twisted ornaments of exactly the same pattern in bronze, or more often in gold, are common during the Middle Bronze Age in the British Isles. As an alternative to quadrangular wire, simple or compound ribbon was sometimes twisted thus (Fig. 16). The composite ribbon employed has a X-shaped section and has been made by bending a strip of gold ribbon at right angles longitudinally, joining two such strips along the keel and then twisting the result. From Great Britain these torques were exported to Brittany, Northern France and probably Scandinavia.

In the last-named country in any case a local series, in which the torsion effect is generally produced by cast ridges, began in the Late Bronze Age. It attained its richest development in that belated Bronze Age that corresponds to the Hallstatt period farther south. By then the torsion was often not continuous in the same direction, but portions of the ring had been twisted in opposite ways (Fig. 17, no. 6). Finger-rings were made in the same style.

Another series of British neck ornaments belonging to the Early Bronze Age is allied in form to the Scandinavian gorgets already described. I refer to the so-called *lunulae* of gold. As their name implies, they are crescent-shaped pieces of thin gold plate. The horns are richly decorated with the rectilinear patterns, so characteristic of the Early Bronze Age throughout Western Europe, and terminate in flat catches. Over

Fig. 16. (1) Gold torque, Scotland, Middle Bronze Age. ⅓
(2) Twisted gold armlet, Scotland, Middle Bronze Age (after Anderson). ½

sixty *lunulae* have been found in Ireland but there are six from Scotland. The latter particularly resemble both in plan and ornament the contemporary jet necklaces found in the same country. It has therefore been suggested very plausibly that the *lunulae* originated in Scotland as metal copies of such necklaces, Ireland being only a secondary centre. Thence in any case they were exported to Wales, Cornwall, Brittany, Scandinavia and North Germany (Fig. 19).

FINGER-RINGS

One of the simplest conceivable metal ornaments is a ring of wire or ribbon to fit on the finger. As bone and stone finger-rings go far back in the Stone Age, early metal copies are only to be expected. They are so widespread as to have little cultural significance, and only a few specialized types need mention here.

The Minoans of Crete, copying the Sumerians and Egyptians, used to mark the ownership of a packet or authenticate inscribed tablets by the impression of a seal. This was at first worn on a string, passing in one class through a loop at the back. During Middle Minoan times the loop was enlarged into a hoop to fit the finger. The oval seal part (technically called the bezel) with its long axis at right angles to the hoop, was of course beautifully engraved like the bead or button seals of gems or ivory. No seals nor signet rings were made by the European barbarians till late in the Iron Age, but in the Late Bronze Age rings of bronze leaf, generally horizontally ribbed, were made of bronze ribbon so trimmed as to be much wider at the side worn on the back of the finger than on the other. Such rings, common in South-west Germany and Switzerland, doubtless imitate Aegean signets.

A truly European ring, common in Central Europe from the Early Bronze Age onwards, was formed of a strand of gold or bronze wire doubled with the ends twisted together, coiled into a little cylinder, like the wire bracelets already mentioned. During the Middle Bronze Age a very handsome ring of bronze ribbon, terminating in opposed spiral disks, characterized the Tumulus culture of Western Germany, South-western Bohemia, Austria and Slovakia (Fig. 15, no. 10). In the Late Bronze Age a more wiry version was in vogue also farther east in the urnfields of Moravia and Hungary.

In Britain we find in hoards of the Middle Bronze Age small coils of massive gold with imitation torsion that may have been worn on the fingers but possibly served as money.

BUTTONS, CLASPS, STUDS AND TUTULI

Even in Early Minoan times, buttons of some perishable material, overlaid with gold, were being worn in Crete. The little convex disks of gold leaf, that once had sheathed them and now alone survive, are each pierced with two thread-holes. Similar hollow button-covers, generally of bronze, appear in Hungary even in the Early Bronze Age, and in the Middle Bronze Age become very plentiful throughout Central Europe. In the Late Bronze Age they were gradually replaced by a more solid button, generally flat, with a cast loop on the back instead of the thread-holes.

Buttons of stone, bone and ivory have a longer history. A very famous type, common all through Western Europe and right up to Scandinavia and the Tisza during the Copper Age, is conical and pierced on the flat side with two holes that converge to meet in a **V**.

Such buttons with **V**-perforation in jet or amber remained popular in Britain during the Early Bronze Age (Fig. 18, no. 2).

Studs of stone, shaped like two disks joined by a short cylinder, were used in a rudimentary form, perhaps as lip-plugs, in prediluvian Mesopotamia and reached Crete even before the local Bronze Age began. A developed variant on this in jet was popular in Britain during the Early Bronze Age. Later metal studs of the same plan were largely manufactured in Scandinavia.

Buckles of jet were employed in Great Britain during the Early Bronze Age. They resemble an oval rod with a longitudinal slit.

For fastening the girdle very handsome clasps were used in Central and North Europe during the Middle and Late Bronze Ages. A pretty form, current chiefly in Würtemberg and on the Upper Rhine, was a hook of doubled wire whose ends were coiled in spiral disks. This was replaced in the Late Bronze Age by a flat metal plate, circular save for a narrow tang that was bent over to form the hook; a loop is attached to the back of the disk at the centre. In the Rhône valley during the latest Bronze Age the type was further elaborated, the tang growing into a richly decorated oval plate, while the original disk, no less ornate, developed three additional hooked tangs.

A very distinctive hook was used by Scandinavian warriors of the Middle Bronze Age for attaching the scabbard to the girdle. The hook is massive, cross-pieces project just below its point and its base is a solid disk.

The girdles themselves might sometimes be all of sheet metal. There is an example in beaten silver from Byblos in Syria. Magnificently engraved girdles of hammered bronze were being manufactured in Upper

Italy at the beginning of the Iron Age, and others occur in the contemporary Bronze Age of Hungary. But normally the girdles were of leather or wool, though often decked with metal ornaments. During the Early Bronze Age of Bohemia hammered metal plates were probably thus employed; they are either shield-shaped or circular with a hollow dome-shaped boss in the centre. They are decorated with engraved triangles arranged in parallel rows or on the circumference of concentric circles. Holes near the rim enabled them to be sewn on. The latter type persists throughout the Middle Bronze Age, spreading to South-west Germany and Scandinavia, to be decorated in each region in the appropriate local style.

Early Bronze Age graves in Lower Bavaria contain extraordinary helical pyramids of coiled bronze wire, executed in a technique already exemplified on a smaller scale in the jewellery from the earliest Sumerian graves at Ur(8) (Fig. 15, no. 11). Copying the helices by casting produced a metal disk with a spike in the centre surrounded by concentric ridges(43). A small bent-over tab projects from the edge of the disk for their attachment to girdles or strings (Fig. 15, no. 12). This "spiked tutulus" is very common in the Middle Bronze Age of Hungary and Central Europe. Scandinavian women wore a similarly shaped ornament on their girdles, but in the North the disk is often very large, 11 inches in diameter, and decorated with spirals (Fig. 17, no. 2). In the Late Bronze Age of the North the size is still further increased, and the central spike becomes a regular little pillar surmounted with a knob. A bar across the base of the hollow pillar provides a means of attachment in lieu of the older thread-holes. Quite possibly the so-called hanging vases of the latest Bronze

Age in Scandinavia are just exaggerations of this type of tutulus (Fig. 17, no 4).

Cones of rolled bronze leaf, or more elaborate versions thereof made by casting, were hung like tassels on the ends of woollen girdles.

Besides stuff and metal plate girdles, double chains were already being worn in Bohemia even in the Early Bronze Age. At that date all the links were just circular rings. In the Late Bronze Age farther west rings alternate with wide links of ribbon.

EAR-RINGS AND LOCK-RINGS

All European ear-rings and hair-rings of any interest go back in the last resort to Mesopotamian types [8]. In the very early Sumerian graves recently excavated at Ur of the Chaldees, Woolley found several forms that constitute the starting-points of our series. The simplest type is a penannular gold ring, one end of which has been hammered out till it is boat-shaped while the other is sharp. The wide end is sometimes decorated with filigree work, at others exaggerated to monstrous proportions and duplicated. Contemporary with these undoubted ear-rings are little open spirals, both ends of which are boat-shaped (Fig. 15, no. 14). They were perhaps twisted in the hair over the ears and may provisionally be termed lock-rings. Identical spiral lock-rings are known from Troy II, the Caucasus, South Russia, Hungary and Central Europe. In the latter region a variant grew up in which one end is bent back upon itself. There are also wiry copies influenced by the contemporary ear-rings.

The simple ear-ring with one boat-shaped end is also found at Troy and in Hungary. At the former site barbaric exaggerations lead to the gigantic basket

Fig. 17. (1) Bronze collar, Denmark, Middle Bronze Age. $\frac{1}{4}$
(2) Bronze tutulus, Denmark, Middle Bronze Age. $\frac{1}{4}$
(3) Bronze tutulus, Denmark, Middle Bronze Age. $\frac{1}{2}$
(4) Hanging vase (tutulus), Denmark, Late Bronze Age. $\frac{1}{6}$
(5) Bronze tutulus, Denmark, Late Bronze Age. $\frac{1}{8}$
(6) Torque with alternating torsion, Denmark, Late Bronze Age. $\frac{1}{6}$
(7) Gold "sun disk", Ireland, Late Bronze Age. $\frac{1}{2}$
(8) Penannular gold ornament, Ireland, Late Bronze Age. $\frac{1}{2}$

ear-rings. These were made by soldering on to gold bars
a series of bent wire coils as shown in Fig. 15, no. 8,
the whole being embellished with rosettes and pendants.
The barbarians of the North, who were ignorant of
solder, imitated the Trojan type in two ways. In
Scotland during the Early Bronze Age the basket was
formed of a bent sheet of thin gold with a hook projecting from one long side. Such ear-rings have been
found as British exports in Belgium and Western
Poland. In the Early Bronze Age of Hungary and
Bohemia the gold wire coils that formed components of
the Trojan baskets were elaborated by themselves to
form the ear-ring (Fig. 15, no. 13). Thence they were
exported to the still Neolithic inhabitants of Denmark
in exchange for amber.

NECKLACES AND PENDANTS

Perhaps as early as Middle Palaeolithic times men
had pierced shells and strung them together as necklaces. Upper Palaeolithic man could also carve very
neat beads out of ivory for the same purpose. The
earliest Egyptians we know, the Badarians, could already
drill stone for beads and soon mastered even such hard
materials as carnelian and turquoise. An extraordinary
variety of beads and amulets were carved out of stone
or ivory. In prehistoric India and Mesopotamia, and
later in Crete and the Cyclades too, stone beads were
soon very popular. Stone beads and amulets based on
East Mediterranean models and bone copies thereof
were then very widely diffused throughout the Mediterranean basin and along the Atlantic coasts to Brittany
and Ireland in the Neolithic and Copper Ages, but had
practically gone out of use before the local Bronze Age
began. Along the Danube valley stone beads had never

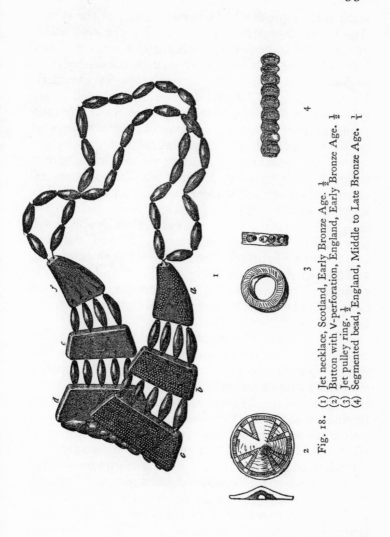

Fig. 18. (1) Jet necklace, Scotland, Early Bronze Age. ½
(2) Button with V-perforation, England, Early Bronze Age. ½
(3) Jet pulley ring. ½
(4) Segmented bead, England, Middle to Late Bronze Age. ⅟₁

come into vogue at all. Hence in a study of the Bronze Age in North-western and Central Europe only amber and jet beads together with a few glazed ones imported from the East Mediterranean need be considered.

Amber necklaces were largely worn in Denmark, Great Britain and Central Europe, going back in the first country to early in the New Stone Age. The most popular form consisted of two or three strings of almost spherical beads connected at intervals by flat spacers. A spacer is a bead perforated with several holes, usually parallel, designed to keep the several strings of a necklace at the proper distance apart. The English and Scottish jet necklaces are similar to the foregoing but often more elaborate. Besides sphericals, thin disks, long barrel-shaped beads and flattened barrels with a little collar at either end were employed, and the spacers were cut to various shapes and diagonally perforated so that the necklace is broader on the throat than behind the neck where it was fastened (Fig. 18, no. 1).

Even the earliest Egyptians could put a glaze on stone beads, and before the beginning of the dynastic epoch they had learned to cast beads of an opaque vitreous material termed faience. The secret had also been grasped in Mesopotamia and India before the beginning of the fourth millennium. Instead of casting a number of separate beads, it was found that the same effect could be obtained more cheaply by moulding a tube divided by grooves into six or eight segments. Thus arose the so-called segmented bead which may have been suggested by the manufacture of simple beads by cutting into segments and then breaking off thin tubular bones or the long roots of bovine teeth. Segmented beads of faience are in any case known from Assur in

Mesopotamia as early as the third millennium B.C., and appear in Crete during M.M. III and in Egypt under the New Kingdom(12). Analogous segmented beads of bluish faience have been found as imports in South-eastern Spain, England (Fig. 18, no. 4) and Poland.

In Mesopotamia metal pendants as well as beads were hung on necklaces. These include gold hoops, bearing wire decorations, and disks engraved and inlaid, in both cases provided with a loop for suspension. We find the same idea applied in Central Europe chiefly during the Middle and Late Bronze Age. A strand of wire, coiled into two spiral disks with a loop between them like spectacles, goes back to the Copper Age, and later a small cast wheel, possibly a solar symbol, became very popular. Another pendant, very common during the Middle Bronze Age in Hungary and adjoining regions as far as the Rhine, is heart-shaped. It is actually inspired by Minoan collar-segments of gold or faience bearing a hybrid pattern, termed by Sir Arthur Evans the sacral ivy-leaf.

Naturally, in addition to the foregoing, simpler ornaments such as marine shells, *Dentalium* tubes, bored teeth and tubes of sheet metal or coiled wire were frequently worn.

VESSELS

Where metal was plentiful, it was used for the manufacture of dishes, cups and ewers and even pails and cauldrons. The majority were made of sheet-metal hammered out. Cups and dishes of precious metals or bronze could be made, as they are to-day, by simply beating up a sheet of metal to the desired shape. For larger vessels two or three sheets were shaped by hammering and then riveted together. Handles too were generally attached by rivets, but in the case of gold and silver vessels they might be soldered on in the Ancient East and the Aegean. Spouts, projecting from the walls of vases in Mesopotamia and Egypt, are said to have been brazed on. Parts of the vessel might receive special treatment. The rim might be strengthened by hammering over it on either side a ribbon of metal. A ring foot can be easily made by inverting the vessel and hammering in a circular depression on the base so as to leave a fold all round, a process termed cupping the base. The handle is normally a piece of ribbon or stout wire with the ends hammered flat to receive the rivets. Metal vessels of varied shape are quite common from the beginnings of the historical period in Sumer and Egypt, at Troy II, in Copper Age graves north of the Caucasus, and in Middle and Late Minoan Crete. North of the Alps none are known before the Late Bronze Age with the exception of two gold cups from Cornwall.

The predynastic Egyptians were very skilled in grinding vases out of even the hardest stones, and stone vessels were also freely used in early Sumer, in Crete from Early Minoan times and in the Cyclades. This material was not adopted for the manufacture of vessels north of the Alps save in Britain. And the small group of English cups of shale or amber, belonging mainly to the Middle Bronze Age, bear no obvious relation to any East Mediterranean form, being equipped with handles and turned on a lathe. Their prototypes are to be sought in woodwork.

Bronze Age pottery exhibits such a variety of forms and ornaments that it must be described in connection with the several cultural groups which it serves to define. Technically, it does not differ in any essential principle from Stone Age wares save in the Ancient East and the Aegean. There the application of the wheel, already described, gave the potter opportunities for all sorts of experiments. In the Aegean too a glaze paint, that is, a paint containing silicates that fuse and vitrify during the firing of the vase, had been invented in Early Minoan Crete and diffused thence to the Early Cycladic and Helladic folk. It enabled the potter to produce lustrous patterns without burnishing the whole surface. Apart from these inventions and even north of the Alps, Bronze Age pottery exhibits some features, notably handles and spouts, apparently unknown or at least very rare in pure Neolithic times.

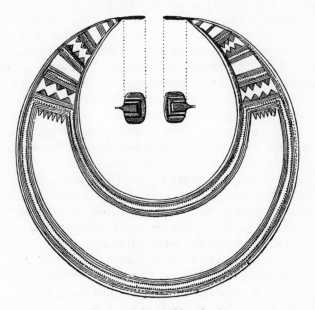

Fig. 19. Irish gold lunula. ¼

CHAPTER IV

THE EARLY BRONZE AGE

THE Bronze Age peoples of Europe were essentially descendants of the stocks inhabiting the same or adjacent parts of our continent in Neolithic times. These were already racially very mixed, and the rise of metallurgy may well have involved the incorporation of foreign artificers and miners in the community, as indicated in Chapter I. Commercial activity, such as necessarily played a prominent part in Bronze Age economics, was also accompanied by a certain interchange of populations, not to be confused with mass migrations. At the same time the dry climatic conditions prevailing facilitated, and in some cases perhaps even necessitated, migratory movements. We thus are faced, even before the beginning of the Bronze Age, with groups already differentiated that by no means lost their identity when they adopted metallurgy. On the contrary, behind the close similarities of bronze tools and weapons that mark the earliest Bronze Age we discern already great divergences in pottery, burial rites and other traits. These divergences soon infect the bronze industry itself. The latter is again differentiated according as Egyptian or Anatolian traditions predominated among the local artificers.

In a general way it seems likely that metal first won general acceptance among the settled farming populations of the coasts and valleys. On the plateaux and plains where forests were giving way to heath and park-land flora, more mobile tribes mainly, though by no means exclusively, pastoral, continued for a while to content themselves with stone tools. Excluding the Aegean and Sicily, there are only three really important centres of Early Bronze Age culture in Europe, namely, Central Europe, South-eastern Spain and Britain, though Upper Italy may be added as a fourth group and the Rhône valley and Brittany were destined soon to join with the other regions.

CENTRAL EUROPE

In the valleys of the Tisza, the Middle and Upper Danube, the March, the Oder, the Upper Elbe and the Saale we find a series of allied communities. They are settled upon the great trade routes connecting the Adriatic with the amber of Jutland and East Prussia, and Bohemia with Slovakian copper and Transylvanian gold. It is convenient to designate all these kindred groups the Aunjetitz cultures, after a great cemetery at Únětice, south of Prague. There are, however, important differences between the several groups in pottery and to some extent also in ornaments. Strictly speaking the Aunjetitz culture is confined to Bohemia, Moravia, Lower Austria north of the Danube, Silesia and Saxo-Thuringia. On the fringe of this area there are local groups named respectively after Gáta on the Austro-Hungarian frontier, Tószeg near Szolnok on the Upper Tisza, Perjámos near Arad on the Maros and Straubing on the Upper Danube in Lower Bavaria (41).

All equally belong to descendants of the local Copper Age populations, essentially Danubian II (Lengyel) folk mixed in varying proportions with intruders from farther north, Anatolians and Bell-beaker folk from Spain. The latter had profoundly affected the industry of the region, without, however, leaving any appreciable trace on the physical character of the population. The metallurgy of our region is none the less on the whole inspired primarily by the Anatolian school as a consideration of the pins and ear-rings at once betrays. From Danubian II times onwards there had been indications of Anatolian penetration in the pottery, Mediterranean shells and stray metal objects found in graves throughout the Danubian area; prospectors, perhaps from Troy, had discovered the gold of Transylvania and the tin of Bohemia. In the advanced Copper Age some ceramic groups exhibit such marked Anatolian features that one suspects a considerable influx of Orientals. Such would presumably have been extracting gold, copper and tin for export down the Danube to Troy where rich bronze occurs in the second city. But when Troy II was sacked, the market would be closed. The strangers must produce for local consumption. The rise of the native Aunjetitz industry dated from that moment.

The Aunjetitz people were of moderate stature but long-headed: they were not therefore descended from the exclusively round-headed Beaker folk. They lived primarily by farming, but undoubtedly controlled the exploitation of ore and the trade in amber and metals. Their dwellings were for the most part round beehive pits dug in the löss, but rectangular houses with plastered wattle walls were also built. The villages were of modest size judging from the cemeteries which comprise no more than a hundred graves. The dead were always interred in the contracted position with the knees drawn up to the breast. In one case in Bohemia a megalithic kist formed the tomb.

Stone and bone tools including celts (some of flint with rectangular cross-section as in the northern Neolithic province), hammer-axes, grooved hammer-stones (p. 6), crescent-shaped flint sickles, bone awls and chisels, horn picks and axes, are quite common in the settlements. From hoards and graves we know flat and flanged celts (both axes and chisels) and quadrangular awls of bronze. The principal weapon was the flat triangular dagger with wooden or bronze hilt, but two bronze battle-axes with knobbed butts have been found in Bohemian graves.

The pins all belong to the group with loop heads, and in particular those with simple roll, knot, perforated globular, racket, disk or husk heads. Distinctive of the Aunjetitz culture in the narrower sense is the pin with a cast loop surmounting an inverted conical head. In all cases the shaft is generally bent near the point. Except for the "manchette" armlet with engraved or ribbed surface, restricted to Bohemia and the immediately adjoining territories, the bracelets are less typical. On the other hand, the ingot torque (Fig. 15, no. 7) is found throughout the area, as are the spiral lock-rings of gold or bronze like Fig. 15, no. 14 and the cognate form of Fig. 15, no. 13. Amber necklaces of two or more strings of beads connected by spacers are common only in Bohemia, Saxo-Thuringia and Bavaria. In Moravia and Lower Austria amber occurs sporadically, while none is reported from Hungarian graves. Tubes of rolled bronze leaf and fossil *Dentalium* shells, together with imported *Cardium* shells or bronze imitations thereof, were likewise strung together for necklaces. Little bone disks decorated with concentric circles may have had a similar use. Girdles of stuff or of multiple bronze chains were worn, and scutiform or circular plates might be sewn on to the former.

The pottery of the whole group is very fine, well

baked and burnished, but rarely decorated. It varies in colour from orange to black and is often mottled like Anatolian wares. The leading form is a mug or jug with a loop handle attached some way below the rim. In the narrower Aunjetitz area it is at first pouch-shaped, having a rather pear-shaped body, a slightly conical neck and an everted rim (Fig. 20, no. 1). The body and neck were moulded separately and then joined, a procedure which leaves a groove round the shoulder. Later the body is suppressed altogether, and we get the classical keeled mug with cavetto neck (Fig. 20, no. 3). In both varieties there is a dimple in the base. The earlier pouch-shaped type alone is found in Bavaria and Lower Austria and recurs with rather longer and narrower neck and a trumpet mouth in the Hungarian Tószeg group. At Per-jámos and Gáta the distinctive type is an hour-glass mug with two handles descending from the brim to the belly— an essentially Anatolian type, that began to appear even in Danubian II. An amphora is also found in Bohemia, but there the handles are attached to the neck below the rim.

Together with the mug goes a wide dish with a groove under the broad brim (Fig. 20, no. 2). There are also a few bowls on hollow pedestals and many large jars or *pithoi* intentionally roughened on the outside. Bohemia and Moravia have also yielded a number of small vases that obviously imitate stone models, imported presumably from the Aegean. Finally from Nienhagen on the northern slopes of the Harz comes a famous clay copy of a Minoan metal cup of the so-called Vapheio shape [12].

Incised ornament when present is limited to a belt of parallel lines round the rim or shoulder with fillets hanging from it. In Hungary the incised lines are replaced by applied ribs arranged in the same way. Small nipples on the shoulders are found everywhere.

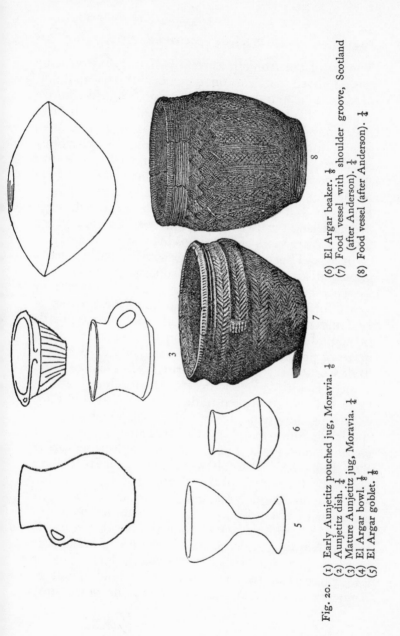

Fig. 20. (1) Early Aunjetitz pouched jug, Moravia. $\frac{1}{6}$
(2) Aunjetitz dish. $\frac{1}{4}$
(3) Mature Aunjetitz jug, Moravia. $\frac{1}{4}$
(4) El Argar bowl. $\frac{1}{8}$
(5) El Argar goblet. $\frac{1}{8}$
(6) El Argar beaker. $\frac{1}{8}$
(7) Food vessel with shoulder groove, Scotland (after Anderson). $\frac{1}{4}$
(8) Food vessel (after Anderson). $\frac{1}{4}$

The art of the Aunjetitz group is better illustrated by the engraved patterns on daggers, armlets and pin-heads. It is purely rectilinear, the favourite motive being a small hatched triangle. On round surfaces these may be arranged in concentric rings. The cross is also found on some disk-head pins. This rigidly rectilinear style is universal throughout the Early Bronze Age save for the Spanish and Scottish stone carvings to be mentioned below. It is sometimes regarded as West European but might equally well be northern, since similar triangle patterns had been very common on the Corded Ware vases of Thuringia in the later Stone Age.

In Saxo-Thuringia side by side with regular Aunjetitz graves distinguished by no superficial monument, we encounter interments under barrows, often very richly furnished. The most famous are the barrows of Leubingen and Helmsdorf. Both contained halberds in addition to the normal Aunjetitz armoury. Such barrows probably belong to descendants of the Neolithic Corded Ware folk of Thuringia. The halberds and a celt of English manufacture from Helmsdorf show that these warriors controlled trade routes leading westward as well as the great amber route along the Elbe. The special culture that was differentiated under these circumstances in the Saale valley may well be no earlier than Reinecke's phase B while the Aunjetitz culture proper occupies both phases A and B.

North of Magdeburg and Glogau no burials furnished with Early Bronze Age types are known. But at least in Scandinavia and along the North Sea coasts the old Nordic population still lived on in a Stone Age burying their dead either in megalithic long kists or under barrows. In a few such graves gold spirals of Aunjetitz types (like Fig. 15, no. 14) or other stray imports have been unearthed to confirm the synchronism of this belated Stone Age with a precocious Bronze culture. Similarly south of the Drave the so-called Slavonian culture seems to lack metal. Yet the pottery includes keeled mugs quite like those of Aunjetitz and Tószeg. Moreover one group of Middle Bronze Age pottery from Hungary is a direct continuation of the Slavonian tradition.

UPPER ITALY

A contemporary centre of metallurgical industry in Northern Italy must be inferred from the distribution of certain types such as the flanged celts like Fig. 4, no. 1. It is not, however, easy to locate the centre accurately. In the province of Brescia extensive cemeteries, notably the type site of Remedello, have been explored that go back to the Copper Age, in fact to the Bell-beaker period. Beside the narrow-shouldered West European dagger and others of Early Minoan form with midrib and short tang and flint copies of both, the graves contained round-heeled triangular daggers and even flanged celts, albeit of pure copper(44).

Within the period covered by the cemeteries pile-dwellings were being founded on the Italian Lakes. These were occupied for a long time and have yielded stone tools as well as Middle and even Late Bronze Age types. But there are indications that some Early Bronze Age forms were actually cast in the lake-villages, and amber beads attest their relations with the North. It is supposed that the lake-dwellers were invaders from beyond the Alps though their precise home is uncertain. Some of the pots really resemble early Aunjetitz shapes, but they exhibit a curious spur or thumb-grip at the top of the handle that is more at home south of the Alps.

The Early Bronze Age culture of Italy is, therefore, still rather vague. Industrially Aegean and Spanish traditions met there—even the halberd is represented in hoards. Ethnically an old native Neolithic stock was overlaid by Bell-beaker elements from Spain and immigrants from beyond the Alps.

SPAIN

As a centre of Early Bronze Age industry South-eastern Spain ranks in importance with Bohemia and even perhaps the Aegean. Here, too, it looks as if the rise of a local Bronze Age coincided with an interruption of relations with the Eastern Mediterranean, which obliged foreign metallurgists, settled round the rich lodes of copper and silver, to produce for a local market. The effects of earlier eastern trade are illustrated by the Copper Age settlements and cemeteries of Los Millares in Almeria and of Palmella in Portugal. At Los Millares the dead were buried in beehive tombs built of stones and roofed by corbelling. Similar, but sometimes even finer, tombs are known from Granada, Andalucia and Southern Portugal. The tombs at Palmella are similarly shaped, but hewn out of the rock. Both types seem to be derived from the Eastern Mediterranean. That is confirmed by the discovery at Los Millares of ostrich-shell beads, pins of hippopotamus-ivory, vases of stone and plaster, painted pottery and bone combs, as well as flat celts, West European daggers, saws, arrow-heads and other copper implements. With the Oriental imports are found also Baltic amber, English jet and French calläis. The pottery in all the above-mentioned tombs includes Beaker ware mingled with undecorated local vases sometimes of Early Minoan or Cycladic form.

Siret(46) believes that these rich tombs belonged to Oriental colonists who had founded trading-posts at points commanding the sea route to the North and the local supplies of ore. He insists that the rarity of gold and silver at this time is due to the fact that the precious metals were exported to the Ancient East and the Aegean, just as in Denmark, when in Late Neolithic times the amber trade with Bohemia was established, that substance, formerly common in every tomb, ceased to figure in the grave inventory. In the Bronze Age culture that succeeded that of Los Millares silver became relatively common and foreign imports correspondingly rare, as might be inferred on the assumption of the interruption of eastern trade.

The chief centre of Early Bronze Age civilization lay in Almeria, the type station being El Argar in that province (45). The same culture spread all along the east coast of the Peninsula to the Pyrenees and is traceable, though in an impoverished form, in Andalucia and Southern Portugal.

Physically the Bronze Age population of South-eastern Spain was mixed. Among the males long-heads and round-heads were represented in approximately equal proportions; the women on the other hand were predominantly brachycephalic.

The El Argar folk were certainly farmers and as surely also metallurgists. Moulds, grooved hammer-stones and slag have turned up in several settlements. The people doubtless exploited the local copper and silver ores, but the supply of tin which had to be imported from Galicia, the Cevennes, Brittany or Cornwall was irregular. None of the tools analysed contained as much as ten per cent., and the majority consist of unalloyed copper. In Almeria the El Argar people

lived on hill-tops defended by great stone walls, sometimes pierced by a postern reminiscent of Mycenae. The
houses were agglomerations of rectangular chambers
with stone foundations for the walls. Some may have
boasted two storeys. The dead were buried, contracted,
within the settlements, among or under the houses,
either in small kists of six thin slabs or in large jars.
Some sarcophagi, hollowed out of stone, are also assigned
to this period. Against a wall in one village was an
altar-like construction embellished with horn-like ends
suggesting a well-known Minoan cult object, the horns
of consecration.

The principal tools are celts, flat or with low flanges,
and quadrangular awls. As weapons were employed
round-heeled knife-daggers, halberds and the bow and
arrows. The daggers, as in the Cyclades, were not
seldom attached to the hilts by small silver rivets. As
noted, the daggers eventually grew into short flat swords.
The halberd, the most distinctive weapon of the peninsula, is already foreshadowed by flint blades from Los
Millares and contemporary sites. The bronze specimens
vary widely in shape: most are symmetrical, some have
very broad butts, the rivets may be quite big and a
broad midrib is frequently used to strengthen the blade.
The arrows were tipped with tanged copper heads,
generally lozenge-shaped and seldom barbed. The type
goes back to the Copper Age culture of Los Millares.
Narrow plaques of schist, perforated at either end, were
probably worn on the wrist by archers as a protection
against the recoil of the bow-string. Elsewhere such
wrist-guards are found in graves with Bell-beakers.

The ornaments are dull in comparison with the
Bohemian. The most interesting is a diadem, an open
circlet of silver or sheet copper, shaped so as to leave

an upright projection in front. Plain rings of silver or bronze wire were worn on the arms and fingers and in the ears. Another ornament for the arm or neck was made from a boar's tusk perforated with a series of holes through which small copper rings were stuck. Beads of rolled copper leaf or coiled wire together with shells were hung on necklaces. There are also a few imported beads of calläis, segmented beads of Minoan or Egyptian faience and imitations thereof in bone. Pyramidal bone buttons with V perforation served to fasten the garments.

The El Argar pottery, like that of Aunjetitz, is normally unornamented and red, black or mottled. Handles are virtually unknown, nor is the base ever dimpled; rounded bottoms are indeed common. The main forms are goblets with inverted rims on a solid pedestal (Fig. 20, no. 5), dishes with similar rims, big carinated bowls with flattened conical necks (Fig. 20, no. 4), and keeled mugs with cavetto necks (Fig. 20, no. 6). The latter closely resemble the Aunjetitz form in profile, but never have handles. Such parallels need imply no direct connection; they are rather developments of Copper Age types in which North African and Aegean elements were prominent, and some of which reached Central Europe along with the Bell-beaker culture.

In the East Spanish cradle of the El Argar culture, so rich in artistic production of the Stone and Copper Ages, no indications of decorative activity assignable to the Bronze Age have come to light. But in the North-west (Northern Portugal, Galicia and the Pyrenees), where isolated bronzes of El Argar form and traces of contemporary mining have come to light, two curious series of rock-carvings exist that may be described here. The first and older group is a degenerate descendant of the well-known Copper Age group described by Burkitt ((1) p. 217). Its patterns seem to represent yet more conventionalized versions of the human figure. The body has become a rectangle or three concentric circles round a central dot. The head is denoted by a vertical line starting from the periphery and sometimes terminating in a circle or a cross. A pair of short oblique strokes, sprouting from the upper corners of the rectangles or the appropriate cords of the circles may be added to represent arms, and legs may be similarly indicated (Fig. 21, no. 1). Some of these figures may stand for the four-wheeled carts depicted on the Copper Age monuments.

In a later group conventionalization had proceeded even farther. Of the old figures nothing now remains but circles sometimes traversed by a radial line and enclosing a round hollow, termed a cup mark (Fig. 21, no. 1), or a group of such. But mixed up with these geometric figures on some rocks are highly conventionalized but quite recognizable animals, carved in the same technique. Apart from these animal figures the later Galician rock-carvings offer most interesting parallels to the "cup and ring" markings of the British Isles. They thus supplement the evidence afforded by beads and tools for the continuance of those ancient trade relations along the Atlantic coasts of which the distribution of megalithic tombs give proof in the Stone Age.

Settlements and cemeteries of classical El Argar type are common only along the east coast of the peninsula from the Ebro to Gibraltar. In Portugal El Argar types occur principally in the late degenerate forms of the local megalithic tombs. The same remark applies to the Pyrenaean region where a local megalithic culture, evolved in the Copper Age out of a fusion of

Portuguese, Bell-beaker and local Neolithic elements, now accepted some El Argar types of tool and pottery. In time the range of the El Argar culture may be considerable. It must begin quite early in the second millennium B.C., yet, at least in its homeland, it has no successor till the Iron Age.

Apart from the limited adoption of El Argar types in the south, it seems that the natives of France were incapable of fulfilling the conditions requisite for regular supplies of metal. Though isolated bronzes of early type are widespread, burials furnished with such are confined to the north-west corner and the extreme east (Savoy and Jura). The negative evidence is supplemented· by the discovery of a few Bronze Age trinkets among Neolithic or Copper Age grave goods in the stone kists of the Cevennes or the *allées couvertes* of the Seine-Oise-Marne basins.

In Normandy and Brittany on the other hand a series of tombs furnished with Early Bronze Age types testifies to a vigorous though belated metal industry. The Armorican culture probably belongs rather to the Middle Bronze Age, like that of the Rhône, and so does not rank as an original centre of metallurgy, but it is none the less more convenient to mention it here at the expense of chronological exactitude. The Bronze Age graves lie conspicuously outside the areas where the famous megalithic tombs are concentrated. They seem to denote a new and probably intrusive culture. The tombs are generally chambers, built of small stones not bonded with any mortar and roofed either with a single large capstone or with a corbelled vault. The whole structure was buried beneath a mound or cairn. Usually no passage connected the chamber with the exterior of the cairn, but some tombs with a corridor of access in

Normandy may belong to this period. The tombs were designed for one interment only, and in most cases the body had been burned, though inhumations occur (51).

The furniture includes flat celts and round-heeled daggers[1] of bronze and superb tanged and barbed arrow-heads of flint. One wooden dagger-hilt had been studded with 1333 little gold nails; other daggers are bronze hilted. Wrist-guards for the bowman have been found but rarely. Among the ornaments may be mentioned a ring-head pin of silver and rare beads of amber or vitreous paste.

A curious vase regularly accompanies these burials. It is strictly biconical though the upper cone is shorter and more depressed than the lower one. Two or four wide strap handles unite the rim to the keel where the two cones join. The vases may be decorated with herringbone incisions or with rows of hatched triangles along the keel and base and the same inverted below the keel and along the rim. This is the same style of decoration that we find generally on bronzes and gold ornaments throughout the Early Bronze Age. The origin of this culture is at the moment unknown.

The Early Bronze Age cultures in Savoy and Eastern France are chiefly represented by burials under barrows which may still contain stone axes (celts) together with bronze offerings. They are inspired partly from Bohemia and Hungary like the Rhône culture of the Middle Bronze Age.

At the close of the Neolithic Age the dominant folk on both sides of the Rhine possessed the culture termed

[1] Déchelette figures as halberds certain blades from S. Fiacre, Morbihan. An examination of the weapons, now in Oxford, disclosed not the straight transverse lines left by a halberd shaft, but the semi-circular plate usually left by dagger hilts.

by Burkitt "Pile-dwelling". They dwelt in fortified settlements. At the same time part of the country was overrun by Corded Ware makers from farther east and the Bell-beaker folk from the West. Mixed communities arose under these conditions. From an amalgamation between the two intrusive groups sprang the so-called Zoned-beaker group. This people already possessed round-heeled daggers of true Bronze Age type. A large proportion of them went down stream and settled in Britain, as we shall see below.

In the Rhineland itself, however, a kindred group, including more Pile-dwelling elements, remained behind and created the Adlerberg culture, so called after a village and cemetery on a knoll of that name on the outskirts of Worms. The huts were pit-dwellings, partly sunk in the earth, and the graves, situated among the huts, each contained a contracted corpse. Round-heads were predominant in the population. The grave goods are poor and primitive—rare flat celts, round-heeled flat daggers and quadrangular awls of bronze, and pins with broad rolled heads and a shaft bent like a sabre. The latter type was also imitated in bone. The graves also yielded flint knives and arrow-heads, bone and allegedly ivory rings, and beads and shells, including Mediterranean species, pierced for stringing.

The commonest pot is a rather biconical or pear-shaped mug with ribbon handles, that may be decorated with rows of incised triangles like the Armorican vases.

GREAT BRITAIN

The round-headed Beaker folk who descended the Rhine settled in Great Britain, introducing there their own habit of individual burial under a round barrow in contrast to the collective interments under a long barrow

practised by the supposedly older "Neolithic" long-
heads. Naturally the invaders from the East did not
exterminate the older population. The latter continued
to bury their dead for a time in the family vaults under
long barrows, and, though the round barrow eventually
became universal, probably ended by absorbing the
intruders. They at any rate played a part in the development of the bronze industry. Yet the oldest metal
objects in Britain have been found under round barrows
and with beakers. Though flint and stone are far
commoner than metal with such pottery, the Beaker
folk probably introduced the knowledge of metallurgy
or the organizing ability needed to make that knowledge
effective; the establishment of the necessary organization
naturally took time for invaders in a strange country.

Our knowledge of the British Bronze Age being
founded in a peculiar degree upon a study of the funerary
pottery and associated grave goods, our account of it
must begin with a description of the main types. The
beakers(1) that symbolize the invaders have been divided
into three main classes by Thūrnam and Abercromby,
denoted by the letters A, B, and C—most unhappily
since, while the A and C beakers are closely allied, the
B beakers are placed in a class apart by ornament and
associations as well as by form.

Beakers of class B stand nearest to the continental
varieties. The rims are everted and the profile forms a
graceful ε curve down to the base. The clay is fine,
often red and generally burnished. The ornament
is arranged in predominantly horizontal zones, as a
rule alternately plain and decorated. The patterns,
repeated round the zones, are quite simple—chevrons,
triangles, X's. The decoration was executed either
with a cog-wheel or short-toothed comb of bone or

wood whose square teeth, rolled over the wet clay, have left an almost continuous series of little rect-angular depressions, or (in North Britain) with a cord impressed upon the damp clay or finally with a simple pointed implement. Beakers of this type are found all over the island. They are regularly associated with bronze, or perhaps copper, daggers of West European type (Fig. 7, no. 2), barbed and tanged flint arrow-heads, stone wrist-guards and buttons with V-perforation, but never with objects of Nordic type (stone battle-axes or flint daggers).

Beakers of types A and C bear a close family likeness. The neck is practically straight or even inturned at the rim and makes a definite angle with the globular body instead of rising out of it in a continuous swelling curve. In type A the neck is relatively long in comparison with the body while in C it is shorter. These beakers exhibit a greater variety of ornament than those of class B. The arrangement is no longer exclusively horizontal; a division into panels or metopes is common, and occasionally vertical bands predominate. The patterns include saltires, elongated triangles and lozen-ges. Cord-impression is not employed, but in addition to the remaining devices applied to the decoration of B beakers, we have the imprint of finger-nails and of a hollow reed or bird's leg-bone. In type C horizontal ridges in relief may be used decoratively. In the same class are to be included a small group of beakers with handles. Such appendages are foreign to the pure bell-beakers of Western Europe, but are not rare in Bavaria and farther east. With beakers of types A and C are associated flat round-heeled daggers with rivets for the handle (Fig. 7, no. 3), flint daggers, stone battle-axes and flint arrow-heads.

Lord Abercromby(53) believed that the Beaker folk landed at one point on our coasts, probably in Kent, and spread gradually northwards. The gradual degeneration of type A would provide a time-scale for checking their advance. The theory of a single landing-place is now generally rejected, and class B beakers must be excluded from the typological series as a group apart. On the other hand, the C beakers, that may well be decadent descendants of the A group, are really commonest in North Britain. So the people who made them may in truth have spread northwards by land routes rather as Abercromby imagined.

Partly, at least, contemporary with the beaker burials are others, accompanied by a quite unrelated vase termed a food vessel. This was the funerary pot of the "Neolithic" stock and originated in North Britain or Ireland out of a bowl found in the long barrows and contemporary settlements. The allegedly Neolithic bowls were round-bottomed so that food vessels showing this peculiarity may be regarded as early. Such are lotus-shaped with ornament even on the base; they are termed type A by Abercromby. Very soon the base was flattened and a groove developed round the widest part of the body (Frontispiece). As a further development, or more probably as a derivative of another variety of "Neolithic" bowl, the part above the grooves was contracted somewhat to form a slightly concave neck, the groove being now in a well-marked shoulder. The classical types of England are a modification of this. The lower part is an inverted truncated cone; above this comes a marked shoulder bearing one (types 1 and 2) (Fig. 20, no. 7) or two (type 4) grooves or none at all (type 3). The shoulder is surmounted by a short concave neck. In all food vessels the rim is broad and moulded, generally on the inside.

Food vessels, especially in North Britain and Ireland, are very richly decorated. The cog-wheel technique, distinctive of Beaker ornament, is indeed comparatively rare on food vessels south of Derbyshire, while cord impressions are exceptional farther north. On the other hand, three methods of ornamentation strange to beakers were freely employed on food vessels in Ireland and Western Scotland, but grow progressively rarer as we proceed southward in England. They are termed by Abercromby the whipped-cord, the looped-cord and the false-relief techniques respectively.

In the first a cord, twisted tightly round a pin or other thin core, is impressed upon the damp clay, a style of decoration known also on "Neolithic" pottery in Scotland. The looped-cord effect may be obtained by twisting two cords together to form a braid which is impressed upon the clay, then unwinding the braid and forming a new one with the cords twisted in the opposite direction. The false relief is obtained by impressing on the soft clay a bone or wooden implement with a triangular point like that of a penknife so as to produce a series of triangles whose bases form a continuous line. The process is repeated with the point of the instrument inverted so as to yield a second series of triangles whose bases shall be parallel to those of the first but whose apices point to the junction of the bases of the first series. A zig-zag band is thus left in relief between the two sets of inverted triangles (Frontispiece). Sometimes an actual triangular stamp of wood may have been employed. And in any case the effect is similar to that of the fretwork technique on Central European pottery described in the next chapter. It is already seen on some true bell-beakers from North Spain and Central Europe.

Though covered with patterns, food vessels seldom exhibit such distinctive motives as are seen on beakers of class A. We may, however, draw attention to the radial cruciform or stellate patterns on the bases of some Irish and Scottish examples. They distinctly recall the patterns radiating from the bases of vases of the bell-beaker class in Spain and Portugal (Frontispiece).

The food vessels of early type are found principally in Ireland and the more mountainous northern and western portions of Great Britain. In Southern England funerary vases of this group are quite rare, and all belong to late or degenerate types. Food vessels, in fact, doubtless belong to the "Neolithic" stock, dispossessed in the south by the Beaker folk. Nevertheless fresh arrivals from the south-west, whence the "Neolithic" people had presumably come, are highly probable. A reinforcement of Spanish influence is demonstrated by the radial decoration mentioned above as well as by the contemporary halberds, the chambered tumuli of the type of New Grange, the carvings on stones there and elsewhere and other cognate phenomena.

With food vessels are associated flat triangular daggers, celts and awls of bronze, flint arrow-heads and stone battle-axes, but no wrist-guards or flint daggers and very few buttons with V-perforation. The skulls of corpses interred with food vessels, like those from the "Neolithic" long barrows, are quite often long-headed in contrast to the pronounced round-headedness of the Beaker folk. Moreover, in some instances food vessels accompany cremated interments and may even contain the ashes.

To adapt them better to the function of ossuaries, the food vessels were eventually greatly enlarged, becoming what are termed cinerary urns. The general adoption of cremation, signalized by the appearance of the cinerary urn, may be conveniently taken to mark the beginning of the Middle Bronze Age here, although no corresponding changes in the buried bronze offerings can be detected. And it must be noted that even beakers were in use side by side with early cineraries.

Sharply defined cultural groups are not distinguishable in Great Britain till the Late Bronze Age, but even in our period we can discern the working of a principle, recently enunciated by Dr Fox[71]. In the predominantly lowland area south-east of a line from Teesmouth to Torquay foreign cultures of continental origin tend to be imposed; in the highland country to the north-west such tend to be absorbed. In our period the Beaker culture maintained itself for a long time in the south; in the north the native Bronze culture characterized by food vessels soon developed and superseded it. Two overlapping phases of the British Early Bronze Age are thus obvious; the first, marked by the earlier types of beakers, witnessed the arrival and expansion of the round-headed invaders; during the second the older population, distinguished by the food vessels, reasserted itself. Thanks to the blending of two traditions the native civilization of the British Isles during these two periods was vigorous and original.

While they undoubtedly cultivated grains and engaged in trade and industry, our Bronze Age ancestors were semi-nomadic. As Dr Curwen[80] puts it "like the patriarch Isaac who 'sowed in that land and found in the same year an hundredfold...and departed thence' our Bronze Age ancestors inhabited a site from one to five years until the cornplots were exhausted and then moved elsewhere". No large villages have been found, and the earlier burials do not constitute regular cemeteries. A few fortified enclosures on hill-tops were certainly occupied by the Beaker folk, but their foundation dates from an earlier age. The defences, of which Windmill Hill near Avebury offers the typical example, consisted of concentric moats interrupted by frequent causeways(108).

The dwellings of the period were mainly circular. In England the hut was excavated in the chalky ground and completed probably by a conical roof of skins. In Scotland beaker sherds have been found in "hut-circles" of which the foundation only—a circular bank of stones and turf—survives; the nature of the super-structure is unknown. In one near Muirkirk in Ayr-shire(79) a post hole was observed near the centre as well as a large hole full of ashes and cracked stones that served as a cooking-pit. Such hut-circles are scattered all over the moors throughout the British Isles and are easily seen when the heather is not too high. In all a gap in the circular bank, often flanked by great stones, marks the doorway. In some later huts (Late Bronze Age) on Dartmoor(78) the megalithic jambs and the stone lintel above them are still in position. These show that by the Late Bronze Age at least the hut with low narrow doorway (2 feet 9 inches wide by 3 feet 9 inches high) was already well established. Sometimes the door opens on to a low narrow passage, often bent in an elbow. A comparison with the snow huts of the Esquimaux suggests that these features were designed to exclude currents of cold air. The superstition about draughts that makes railway travelling so painful even now is clearly very old. The inhabitants of hut-circles seem to have enjoyed the odorous warmth of human bodies clustered about a reeking fire as much as their Arctic representatives. The stone hut-circle, with its analogues in the beehive tomb, is an Atlantic-Mediterranean device inherited from the old "Neolithic" stock in Britain, but it continued to grow into even more elaborate forms during the Iron Age.

Hut-circles generally occur in little groups, evidently tiny hamlets of from four to twelve families. Adjacent to some groups, for instance on Dartmoor and on Spartleton Edge in the Lammermoors, remains of irregular enclosures, fenced by dry walls of stone, are noticeable. They may denote the cornplots of the semi-nomadic villagers(80).

Nearly all Early Bronze Age burials have been marked externally by a mound of earth or a cairn of stones. But the barrows and the grave beneath them vary considerably in structure. The simplest form of barrow is a roughly circular mound; from their external appearance such tumuli are termed "bowl barrows". The base of the mound is sometimes surrounded with a ring of large stones, technically called a peristalith, that served to keep the material of the tumulus in place. Occasionally such a ring of stones or a circular trench dug in the virgin soil encircles the grave but is completely buried by the mass of the barrow. Very close attention is therefore needed during the excavation of even a simple bowl barrow to disclose these and other possible structural features. A more elaborate monument is the so-called "bell barrow". Here the mound is surrounded by a ditch or fosse with a bank outside it; a narrow belt of level ground, known as the berm, generally intervenes between the inner lip of the encircling fosse and the base of the mound proper. Some gigantic tumuli, covering built chambers, such as the celebrated Maes Howe in Orkney, could be classed as bell barrows though some believe them to be Neolithic rather than Bronze Age. In a third type, christened the "disk barrow", the central eminence has virtually disappeared; we have, that is, an immense berm encircled by fosse and rampart. Such are supposed to be late in the Early Bronze Age; disks are generally earlier(72).

The normal grave of the Beaker people was a simple trench or, in hard country, a short kist built of six stone slabs at the centre of the barrow. In Ireland and Northern and Western Scotland some round cairns which covered circular or more often cruciform chambers, roofed by corbelling, are still assigned to the Bronze Age. Such chambered cairns are clearly connected with the old long barrows that covered similar chambers. And it must be remembered that Early Bronze Age pottery, principally Beaker ware, has been found in quite a number of long barrows, showing that such family vaults were still in use when the Beaker folk reached our shores.

"The standing stones on the naked wine red moor" are a feature of British highland scenery scarcely less impressive than the grandeur of their setting. Mr Burkitt(1) has already described the principal characters of *menhirs*, alignments and cromlechs as well as Stonehenge(75), but a few additional words on the stone circles are indispensable to any account of the Bronze Age in Great Britain. It has been suggested that the stone circle developed out of the peristalith of a cairn or from the buried setting under one(73). At Clava near Inverness we actually find circles of huge upright stones enclosing the chambered cairns, and at Callernish in Lewis a similar ring of uprights encloses a chambered tumulus but just touches its periphery. Our stone circles vary widely in character and doubtless also in date and function. All consist of upright stones placed so as to form a ring, but the number, size and arrangement of the stones are variable. There are circles whose stones barely emerge above the surface of the ground and others like Avebury (Wilts), consisting of stupendous blocks of stone. Some large circles are surrounded by a fosse and bank like the Rings of Brodgar (no bank) and Stennis in Orkney, Arbor Low in Derbyshire and of course Stonehenge itself and Avebury. The diameter between the stones of Brodgar is 340 feet. A much smaller example of a similar type (without bank) is to be seen at the Broomend of Crichie near Inverurie with a diameter of only 38 feet. Its six pillars surround a central burial kist. In a specialized group, confined to Aberdeenshire, the uprights increase in height progressively throughout a semicircle, and a huge horizontal slab, termed the recumbent, lies between the two highest which are of course adjacent. Some circles at least were sepulchral. For example, a kist containing a food vessel was found so precisely in the centre of a circle on Mauchrum Moor on the west coast of Arran that grave and circle must have been conceived as a single monument. The food vessel incidentally fixes the Early Bronze Age date of this circle at least. But others may be later in date and need not have been connected with any burials. Sometimes two circles are closely juxtaposed as in the famous Grey Wethers on Dartmoor.

Near many stone circles stands a single upright termed the outlier. Such are attached to all sorts of circles in all parts of the country, e.g. to the fossed Ring of Brodgar in Orkney, to most Aberdeenshire circles, to the small ring termed the Rollright Stones in

Oxfordshire, etc. Outliers furnish one of the principal arguments to those who believe the circles to have been astronomical. The outlier would be a pointer to mark some celestial event viewed from the centre at a stated season of the year. Unfortunately in quite a number of cases the only possible phenomena to which many of these outliers might have been orientated prove to be of such an inconspicuous nature that they are unlikely to have attracted attention in our clouded heavens. Indeed it is fantastic to imagine that the ill-clad inhabitants of these boreal isles should shiver night long in rain and gale, peering through the driving mists to note eclipses and planetary movements in our oft-veiled skies.

The cover-stones of certain Scottish kists containing food vessels or beakers exhibit a curious carved decoration, and allied patterns can be seen on the stones of the peristaliths and chambers of the famous chambered tumuli at New Grange and Lough Crew in Ireland. Here Professor Breuil has been able to distinguish four series(1). The first, simple engraved lines, and the second, consisting of spirals and other curvilinear figures executed by pocking, are anterior to the building of the tumuli which partly hide the markings. Subsequently other patterns—lozenges and diapers pocked all over—were squeezed into the spaces left by the earlier figures. Designs of the same series, Breuil's group IV, recur together with spirals, on the underside of the stone covering a kist containing a beaker at Carnwath in Lanarkshire (Fig. 21, no. 2). Between these limits fall a large series of patterns, allied in design and technique to group II but executed on living rock surfaces in Southern Scotland and Northern England. The commonest device here is the "cup-and-ring marking": a shallow depression, 1–2 inches in diameter hammered

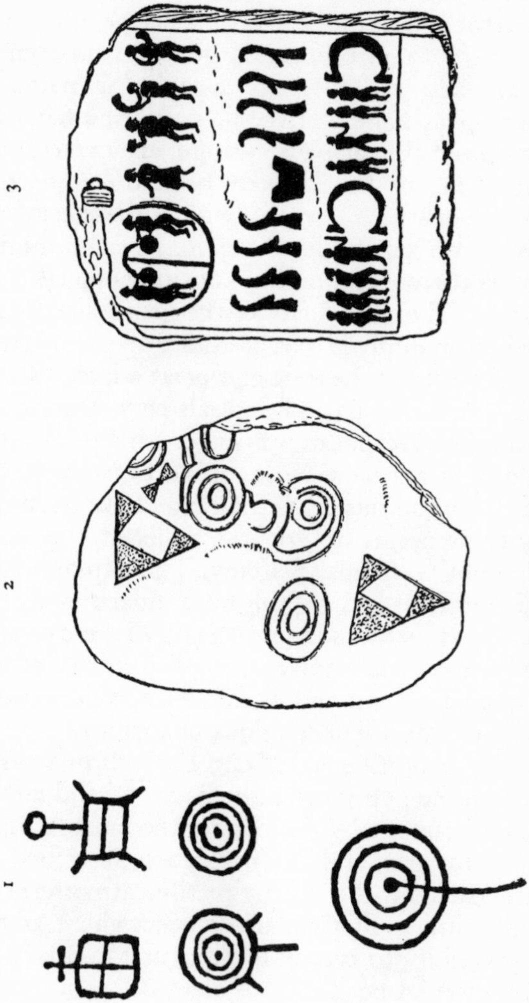

Fig. 21. (1) Conventionalized human figures carved on rocks of Galicia.
(2) Coverstone of a kist at Carnwarth, Lanarkshire.
(3) Slab from the tomb at Kivik, Sweden.

out in the rock surface, is surrounded by from one to eight concentric circles, pocked out; a groove often runs from the centre to just beyond the outermost circle (cf. Fig. 21, no. 1). Cognate curvilinear patterns, showing very clearly the motive of a pair of human eyes that is just discernible at New Grange, are carved on a chalk drum found under an Early Bronze Age barrow at Folkton in Yorkshire. Probably in all these carvings we have very conventionalized versions of the human figure or parts thereof and perhaps of ritual objects such as bull-roarers. The peculiarity of the group lies in the use of curvilinear motives that are otherwise foreign to the Bronze Age art of Europe except at a later date in Scandinavia and Hungary. The spirals have been interpreted as due to Mycenaean influence. In any case the carvings do indicate very close connections with the South-west. The spirals of New Grange have parallels, which cannot be accidental, on the walls of the great passage grave of Gavr'inis, Brittany. The cup-and-ring markings exhibit no less significant similarities to the Galician carvings mentioned on p. 150. These carvings can hardly be merely decorative. As we have no insight into their inner function and significance, we mask our ignorance by calling them religious or magical.

The purely decorative art of our Early Bronze Age is illustrated on the pottery already discussed and on the weapons and ornaments. Of the latter the most striking are the gold lunulae and jet necklaces described in Chapter III. All show the strictly rectilinear patterns of triangles and similar motives usual everywhere at the period, engraved in the case of bronzes and lunulae and punctured on the jet beads.

The main types of tools and weapons in use have already been sufficiently summarized in dealing with the grave goods associated with beakers and food vessels. The only important addition to the list, given by a study of the few hoards assignable to the period, is the halberd that was, as noted in Chapter III, very common in Ireland. It must again be insisted that flint was very freely used, not only for arrow-heads but also for all sorts of knives and scrapers, and polished stone celts, as well as battle-axes, were still current. Yet copper or bronze flat celts were manufactured locally. Moulds for casting such have turned up in Scotland to an extent unsurpassed anywhere on the continent outside South-eastern Spain, and the distribution of actual specimens coincides fairly closely with that of Early Bronze Age settlement as disclosed by Beaker burials. On the other hand, Dr Fox(89) contends that the bronze knife-daggers were imported from the South by sea. They are certainly concentrated in South-western England and become disproportionately rarer to the east and north. Commercial or other connections with the Iberian Peninsula were certainly close during the period. And a dagger whose wooden hilt was decorated with tiny gold nails affords a link with contemporary Brittany. At the same time contact with the lands across the North Sea is illustrated by the amber necklaces and flint daggers of Scandinavian type as well as by beads in the form of a double-axe—a well-known "Neolithic" type in Denmark.

Thus three currents met in England during the Early Bronze Age—one from Central Europe represented by the invading Beaker folk, another from the Iberian Peninsula, perhaps unconnected with popular movement, and a third, plainly mercantile, from Scandinavian countries. That explains the intense vigour and originality of our Bronze Age civilization.

CHAPTER V

THE MIDDLE BRONZE AGE

THE Middle Bronze Age is much more than a mere continuation of the previous period. It witnessed the rise of schools of metallurgy in regions where Early Bronze Age types are rare and among peoples who had spent the preceding period in a belated Stone Age. The new communities of metal-workers made an original contribution to the common European stock of types. Thus many of the bronzes illustrate a new spirit instead of being just improvements on the older types. Conversely, in several centres of early metallurgy, particularly South-eastern Spain and Great Britain and to some extent also Central Bohemia, Middle Bronze Age types are either totally lacking or represented only by stray objects and a few hoards. The principal new provinces are Scandinavia, the South-west German uplands and Hungary, to which may be added the peculiar developments in Upper Italy and the Rhône valley. It will be seen from a glance at the map that these centres lie along and on either side of the great central amber route. The regions remote therefrom failed to participate in the new developments.

SCANDINAVIA

While the earlier Aunjetitz culture had been flourishing in Bohemia, and plentiful metal objects were being buried with beakers and early food vessels in Great Britain, the peoples of Scandinavia and North Germany still used stone tools, supplemented by a very few bronzes imported from England or Central Europe. To that epoch should be assigned the latest megalithic kists and the separate graves high up in the barrows of the Battle-axe folk. The latter had obtained complete dominance before the secrets of metal-working had been mastered locally. But smiths were eventually attracted to Denmark, which became the centre of a new metal-working province, termed Germanic or Teutonic. Besides Denmark it embraced the Norwegian coasts, Southern Sweden, North-west Germany and Central Germany north of Magdeburg.

The distribution and grouping of the barrows—for very few settlements are known—produces the impression of a semi-nomadic people, living in little groups with a limited regular range. It must be remembered that the dry sub-boreal conditions had converted the North European plain into an open park-land, verging on steppe in some districts. The Bronze Age population buried their dead, like the Neolithic Battle-axe folk, under barrows, normally in the extended position and very often enclosed in coffins formed out of hollowed oak trunks.

Besides flint tools—sickles, scrapers, knives, and even celts—flanged celts, palstaves or even socketed celts, button sickles and knives were manufactured locally in bronze. In men's graves weapons are abundant. From such come the splendid swords with inlaid pommels, great socketed spear-heads sometimes 35 cm. long, and, more rarely, heavy battle-axes with a shaft-hole. The arrows were still tipped with flint points, and even flint daggers remained current, though inferior in workmanship to the amazing products of the last Neolithic Period.

Unusually favourable circumstances have preserved to us substantial vestiges of the actual clothing then worn. Men wore a close-fitting woollen cap; a sort of blanket was girt round the body under the arms, while the shoulders were covered with a plaid fastened by a brooch at the throat. Women were clad in a short sleeved jacket, like a pull-over, and a skirt formed by girding a blanket round the waist. Their long hair was held in place by a net. Both sexes were shod with leather boots. The simple woollen dress was set off by a wealth of gold or bronze ornaments. For fastening the cloak two-piece fibulae (Fig. 14, no. 16) were used, but neat studs were also manufactured. The leather girdles were fastened with the clasps already described on p. 127 and decked with tutuli. These are circular. Those worn by women have a central spike while the disk may attain a diameter of 28 cm. (Fig. 17, no. 2). Men's were of more modest size with a hollow boss or *umbo* in the centre. Males wore bracelets on the left arm only, females on both. The most distinctive and beautiful terminate in spirals or pairs of spirals. Finger-rings and bracelets of double gold wire were favoured by both sexes. Finally, women wore the broad gorgets, like Fig. 17, no. 1. Necklaces of amber or glass beads are less common.

Towards the close of the period toilet articles in the form of tweezers, single-edged razors (Fig. 12, no. 11) and bronze combs begin to appear in the graves.

Pottery is rare and exceedingly rough. Finer vessels were made of wood. Several neat cups of this material have survived. They appear to have been turned on a pole-lathe, are provided with a band handle and sometimes are adorned with little tin nails forming a star pattern on the base.

The Teutons of the Middle Bronze Age displayed high artistic capacity. Their aesthetic taste is best exemplified in the shapely weapons and graceful ornaments and their decoration. Axes, sword-hilts (Fig. 9, no. 6), collars and tutuli are covered with running spiral patterns engraved with astonishing accuracy. In the later phases of the Bronze Age the first delicacy is lost, but we shall see a fine revival of curvilinear ornament in the latest period that corresponds to the southern Hallstatt age.

Probably to our period belong also some rock-engravings, found principally in Bohuslan, Southern Sweden. As artistic productions they are far inferior to the delicate geometrical art of the bronze-worker or to the older naturalistic engravings of the Arctic Stone Age hunters (Burkitt (49), p. 2 1 3), but they are none the less full of human interest. They depict in fact scenes of daily life—men at the plough, combats between warriors protected by round shields, very like those we shall meet in the Late Bronze Age, and naval battles between great rowing galleys. Different in style from the foregoing are the engravings on a Middle Bronze Age grave kist unearthed at Kivik, Schönen. One slab depicts a prince in a chariot, directing the slaughter of three naked captives quite in the spirit of certain early Sumerian scenes. Another slab (Fig. 21, no. 3) represents some rather puzzling ritual ceremonies: its upper register shows a band of musicians blowing long curved trumpets or playing other less easily recognizable instruments; below in the middle we see eight women (looking very like seals!) grouped symmetrically about a large cauldron. The bottom register is taken up with another group of captives being slaughtered.

The significance of these uncouth carvings cannot be over-estimated. They afford the oldest positive proof of the use of wheeled vehicles north of the Alps and probably also of the domestication of the horse. The use of the musical instruments, well known in the succeeding period, is here dated back well into the second millennium B.C. The cult scene is even more important; for it anticipates a ceremony described by Strabo as observed among the Cimbri who hailed from Denmark, and more clearly depicted on a famous bronze cauldron of later date discovered at Gundestrup in Jutland. The Greek author describes how among the Teutonic tribe a priestess used to cut the throats of prisoners of war so that their blood gushed into a great cauldron. Omens were obtained in this manner. The Kivik monument implies a similar gruesome rite among the ancestral Teutons about 1400 B.C., unrolling in salutary wise a blood-stained page which we should gladly forget.

The free use of the spiral, and especially of interlacing spiral figures exactly as at Mycenae, has been thought to betoken Aegean influence, the Irish and Scottish carvings being sometimes invoked as links. But in point of fact the Teutonic Bronze Age was singularly original and independent. Hungary, indeed, supplied models for a number of types, but imported foreign commodities are rare. Of course the metals, copper, tin and gold, had to be imported from the South or West, but they arrived raw and even unalloyed. Of foreign manufactures we find from the East Mediterranean glass beads, from Italy a sword with lead solder on the hilt and from South-west Germany wheel-head pins, but that is all. Conversely Teutonic bronzes were never exported at this date. Save for a couple of two-piece fibulae from the Tyrol and North Italy, the unmistakable bronzes we have described only found their way very sporadically just across the border of the Teutonic province into Holland and Thuringia. The imported metals must have been paid for entirely in amber or slaves. In the Late Bronze Age we shall find affairs changed and Teutonic manufactures reaching Hungary and Switzerland.

THE TUMULUS BRONZE CULTURE

The heaths and upland country of Holland, Western Germany, Bavaria, Upper Austria and South-western Bohemia are dotted over with groups of barrows whose furniture marks each as just a specialized manifestation of a single culture. In the enormous area local differences are only to be expected, and in fact extend to tools and weapons as well as vases and ornaments. Still it is convenient and justifiable to treat all the local groups together as the Tumulus Bronze culture.

The tumulus-builders are thought by many authorities to have been Kelts, but this, as we shall see, is dubious. Physically they were distinctly mixed, including both long-heads and round-heads as well as mesaticephals. But they were the direct descendants of the peoples who had occupied the South-west German uplands and the Alpine slopes towards the close of the Stone Age. Among these the Battle-axe folk, as in the North, would have been the most prominent. Indeed in Upper Bavaria(85), Alsace(86) and elsewhere in the area barrows with Corded Ware have been found in or near the Middle Bronze Age cemeteries, forming as it were their nuclei. These highlanders and heathmen learned metal-working late, like their Scandinavian relatives, and learnt it from the Danubian school, as the earliest bronzes even in Alsace and the French Jura prove.

Economically the barrow-builders must have been largely pastoral and semi-nomadic. There is no doubt that they cultivated grain like our own ancestors, but they did not settle in the fertile valleys like the Aunjetitz folk. Their favourite haunts were poor and hilly regions that are to-day heavily timbered unless artificially cleared, but that under the dry sub-boreal conditions were heath or park-lands, as surviving xerophilous plants indicate. As characteristic regions we might mention the swampy tract of alluvial sands, covered to-day with oak woods, north of Haguenau, near Strasburg, and the lovely slopes of boulder clay above the little glacial lakes behind Munich.

Owing to their mode of life and perhaps under stress of periods of real drought, the tumulus-builders spread far. From centres in Upper Bavaria or Würtemberg the slopes of the Hercynian forest in Bohemia were early colonized, and by the Late Bronze Age we find allied groups as far away as Bosnia. So, too, from the terraces above the Upper Rhine and the Jura the greater part of Eastern and Central France was overrun as far as Charente.

Settlements are practically unknown, but the graves are distinctive. The burial place is always marked by a tumulus of earth or stones generally covering one or two interments only, but sometimes serving as a collective sepulchre. The remains were laid, not in a trench, but just on the surface of the earth, protected by stones. The normal rite was inhumation in the extended position. But cases of cremation occur among even the earliest Bronze Age interments as under Neolithic barrows in the same area. This rite became increasingly common as time advanced. But the ashes were generally just deposited on the ground; only where the influence of the Urn-field folk, described in the next chapter, was strong in the Late Bronze Age, were the ashes enshrined in cinerary urns.

The warrior was armed with an axe, a dagger, and a

rapier or a spear with socketed head. The axe-heads never possessed shaft-holes, but consisted of flanged celts (everywhere), very slender winged celts (Fig. 4, no. 2) (Würtemberg and Upper Bavaria), palstaves (Fig. 3, no. 5) (South-west Germany and Holland) or Bohemian palstaves (Fig. 4, no. 4) (in the Palatinate and Bohemia). The daggers were very seldom mounted in bronze hilts, but at least in Bavaria bronze-hilted rapiers are common. As a defence, the warrior carried a round targe of wood or leather, studded with hollow bronze knobs which alone have survived. The bow was used in hunting, and bronze arrow-heads have been found even in women's tombs though they are far from common. Sickles too of the button type (Fig. 13, no. 1) were sometimes buried in the graves, but, with the possible exception of a small group in Franconia and Bavaria, single-edged knives appeared first in the Late Bronze Age.

The dress was probably similar to that worn in Denmark. Men fastened the cloak at the throat with a single pin; women always used two crossed on the breast. In Würtemberg the type with an eyelet in the swollen neck was at first the standard, to give place in the Late Bronze Age to giant forms with ribbed necks (Fig. 14, no. 10). In Bavaria and Bohemia mushroom-headed varieties were popular, while in Alsace the nail-headed type was once general, though later superseded by wheel-headed and ribbed types. Bracelets were worn by both sexes, exactly as in Denmark. The most general type was a simple rod, tapering at both ends and bent into an open ring, but forms like Fig. 15, nos. 3 and 4, and, on the Rhine, cylinders were quite popular. Finger-rings with ribbon bodies like Fig. 15, no. 10 were displayed upon the fingers, and the legs were sometimes burdened with anklets like Fig. 15, no. 6. Such were an Alsatian speciality. From the Rhine they spread westward into East-central France, helping to mark the expansion of the Tumulus culture. The girdle might be fastened with a spiral-ended hook and was studded with hollow bronze buttons, small spiked tutuli and, later, wheel-pendants. Strings of amber and glass beads, bronze wire coils and pendants including the sacral ivy leaf, were hung round the neck though ingot torques were sometimes worn.

The pottery, often very graceful, varies materially from region to region. But the best proof of the fundamental homogeneity of the whole culture is the fact that any given local ware is represented by stray specimens in almost all the other regions. In the Rhine valley, Würtemberg and Upper Bavaria the commonest shapes are hemispherical cups, jugs with globular bodies and wide funnel-like necks, and big urns with short necks and handles on the shoulders. In Bohemia and the Palatinate the bowls may have pedestals and a handle, the jugs bear four warts on the belly, and the urns are squat with conical necks. The ornamentation is also different. None the less pedestalled bowls quite comparable to the Bohemian are found also in Alsace.

The vases from Bohemia and the Palatinate are decorated either by simply roughening the surface or with incised hatched triangles or chevrons of cross-hatched ribbons. Roughening was also used decoratively in Würtemberg and the other groups, but conical warts sitting on the shoulders are a common decorative device (Fig. 22, no. 1). The most distinctive of all, however, is the so-called fretwork ornamentation (*Kerbschnitt*). The effect at first was similar to the "false relief" on British food vessels, but in this case the little triangles and

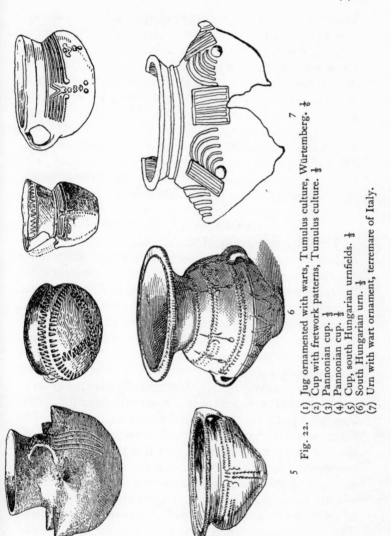

Fig. 22. (1) Jug ornamented with warts, Tumulus culture, Würtemberg. ⅙
(2) Cup with fretwork patterns, Tumulus culture. ⅓
(3) Pannonian cup. ⅓
(4) Pannonian cup. ⅓
(5) Cup, south Hungarian urnfields. ⅓
(6) South Hungarian urn. ⅓
(7) Urn with wart ornament, terremare of Italy.

lozenges were actually cut out of (excised from) the soft clay (Fig. 22, no. 2). Later, stamps of various shapes including circles came into use. In either case the fretwork patterns are arranged, as on beakers, in zones or radiating from the bases of vessels. Fretwork pottery is particularly common in Würtemberg(43) and on the Upper Rhine but is represented also even in Bohemia and Upper Austria, all down the Rhine and right across France to the Departments of Gard, Puy-de-Dôme and Charente. Similarly jugs or urns with conical warts of Swabian style are found in Bohemia and in Western Lorraine (Dept. Meurthe et Moselle(4)).

THE ITALIAN TERREMARE

The third new group of the Middle Bronze Age had its seat in Upper Italy, south of the Po. It is distinguished by a curious sort of settlement termed a *terramara*, the "black earth", full of organic refuse, having been used as fertilizer by the local peasantry. A *terramara* is a low, oblong mound, 12–15 feet high, formed by the debris of prolonged occupation. On exploration it is found that the settlement had been fortified and laid out on a regular plan, common to most sites. The occupied area, which may cover nearly 200,000 square metres (50 acres), is always trapezoid in shape and is surrounded by a moat, 15–25 yards wide and about 12 feet deep. The moat was traversed by a single bridge and could be flooded by a canal joining it at the acute angle of the trapezoid. Some 20 yards inside the moat rises a broad rampart of earth, sloping on the outside but supported within by a wooden construction, resembling a series of small log-cabins and termed in Italian the *contraforte*. The area thus enclosed reveals on excavation a regular forest of piles. These it is supposed supported the actual huts which would have been "pile-dwellings on dry land". They appear to be grouped along lanes parallel to the long sides or at right angles thereto. On the south side there is generally an earthen mound encircled by an inner moat.

Two cemeteries were normally attached to each *terramara*; they are miniature *terremare* with moats of their own. The inhabitants of the *terremare* (termed *terremaricoli*) burned their dead, preserving the ashes in cinerary urns. These are found packed close together in the necropoles.

The *terremaricoli* were prosperous farmers. The number of sickles or moulds for their manufacture testify to the importance of agriculture. The domestication and employment of horses is attested by cheekpieces from bits. But the *terremaricoli* were also skilled craftsmen and keen traders. Metallurgy is illustrated by numerous stone moulds, weaving by whorls, loomweights and spools of clay. Trade brought them, besides metals, amber from the Baltic and glass beads from the Eastern Mediterranean.

Polished stone celts and axes, flint knives, scrapers, arrow-heads and even daggers are not uncommon in a *terramara*, and tools of bone and horn are varied and plentiful. The distinctive bronze tools are flanged and winged celts, flat chisels, little awls, and needles, numerous grooved sickles, and a few single-edged knives. The warrior carried flat triangular daggers with bronze or horn hilts of ogival forms as well as three types of sword—the short sword with flat blade that is just an elongation of the flat dagger, a rapier of continental form, and another with a short tang formed by the prolongation of a pronounced midrib which is derived directly or through Sicily from Minoan types. Odd ogival blades with a short flat tang and projecting shoulders may have been hafted as daggers or as spear-heads. But socketed spear-heads were also in use.

A great variety of pins were worn. Wiry headed varieties, singly or doubly looped and blossoming into spirals and double spirals, are the most distinctive. Little bone wheels that are common may also have been pin heads. Safety-pins of the violin-bow form are late and rare in *terremare*. But double-edged razors were in regular use and cast locally (Fig. 12, no. 5). Another toilet article was a comb of bronze or bone.

Terramara pottery is characterized above all by the extraordinary crescentic or horn-like projections that surmount the vase handles (*ansa lunata, ansa cornuta*). Such are just exaggerations of a feature, found earlier on Italian pottery, to which there are analogies in Macedonia, Aetolia, Malta, Sicily and Sardinia. The shapes include shallow cups, pedestalled vessels, and inverted conical or biconical urns, generally without necks. Warts, pinched out of the clay and often encircled by incisions, are the principal decorative device.

An approach to plastic art is seen in rude clay figurines and models of animals. The bone combs, disks and hilts are often richly carved with zig-zags, triangles, concentric circles or even running spirals.

An important school of Italian prehistorians, founded by the late Professor Pigorini, hold that the *terremaricoli* were the original Italici from whom the Umbrians, Latins and Sabines were alike descended. A genuine *terramara* near Taranto and other more ambiguous remains from Central Italy would be the monuments of the "Aryanization" of the peninsula. It is at least certain that the *terramara* industry became dominant throughout its whole length. According to Pigorini these Italici would have been invaders from beyond the Alps. But despite general analogies in sites like Tószeg on the Tisza, no genuine *terremare* have been found in the Danube basin, and the exact starting-point of the Italici remains uncertain.

HUNGARY

The Middle Bronze Age in Hungary begins with the desertion of several Early Bronze Age sites and a break in the ceramic record—a layer yielding no potsherds—in others. Yet by the end of the period we find the whole plain occupied by extensive communities, each traceable by their pottery to Early Bronze Age groups though the traditions are now differently blended. At the same time a number of bronze types, found stray or in hoards and dated by their context abroad, show that Hungary was now the seat of a very vigorous and original bronze industry.

The most distinctive forms of the period are the shaft-hole axes described on p. 75 above (Fig. 23, no. 1); for celts were not manufactured locally to serve as axe-heads. The forms are probably derived from Copper Age models; the distribution suggests that they were manufactured principally in North-east Hungary, the copper being derived presumably from the Mátra Mountains. Thence they were exported as far as Upper Austria, Bavaria, Mecklenburg, the Ukraine and Serbia. Besides an axe the Hungarian warrior carried a spear with socketed head or—very rarely—a rapier. Small ogival daggers are occasionally found in the late graves. Few tools can safely be assigned to the Middle Bronze Age, but the ornaments were varied and distinctive, and enjoyed a wide popularity even outside Hungary. Many

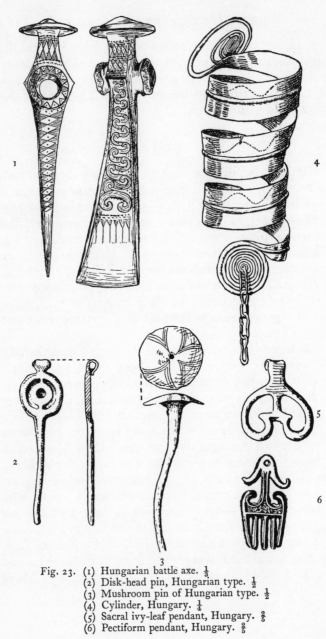

Fig. 23. (1) Hungarian battle axe. $\frac{1}{3}$
(2) Disk-head pin, Hungarian type. $\frac{1}{2}$
(3) Mushroom pin of Hungarian type. $\frac{1}{2}$
(4) Cylinder, Hungary. $\frac{1}{4}$
(5) Sacral ivy-leaf pendant, Hungary. $\frac{2}{5}$
(6) Pectiform pendant, Hungary. $\frac{2}{5}$

Early Bronze Age types of pin remained in use throughout the Middle Bronze Age. But the most characteristic native type had a mushroom head vertically pierced (Fig. 23, no. 3) or with a lateral eyelet just below it. The bracelets tended to be massive and richly engraved. The ends are either thickened or coiled into opposing spiral disks (Fig. 15, no. 3). Hardly less distinctive are the cylinders of bronze ribbon ending in wire spirals worn on the legs and arms (Fig. 23, no. 4).

A great variety of pendants were sewn on the girdle, strung on necklaces, twisted in the locks or hung down over the breasts or the middle of the back. Most are of bronze, but gold specimens are known. Besides the hollow buttons and spiked tutuli, common also in other regions, many varieties of the sacral ivy-leaf pendant were manufactured in Hungary and exported thence as far as Alsace. Another important form is the pectiform or comb-shaped variety that formed a sort of tassel to ornamental chains hung down the back (Fig. 23, 5, 6). The gold spiral lock-rings, current already in the Early Bronze Age, continued to be worn.

Great aesthetic taste was shown by the Hungarians both in the grace of their ornaments and in the magnificent patterns engraved upon their weapons. In North Hungary in particular, scrolls luxuriate over the blades and butts of axes as lavishly as the more austere spirals of contemporary Teutonic art (Fig. 23, no. 1).

The remains from the relatively sterile layer at Tószeg suffice to show that even in the first half of the Middle Bronze Age the Hungarians had at their command the motive power of horses. Apart from these layers and a few inhumation burials, connected deposits are rare as if there had been a considerable exodus at the end of the Early Bronze Age. The lacuna may be the reflex of the abruptly appearing invaders of Italy described in the last section as the *terremaricoli*. Nevertheless before the period closes the abundant remains must betoken a large and settled population, descended from old local stocks. We rely for our information chiefly upon cemeteries which may be divided by burial rites and pottery into several groups. In the largest group termed Pannonian, extending from the Austrian borders south-eastward into Central Hungary, as well as in the cemeteries of the Banat and North-east Serbia that continue the same line, cremation was the sole rite observed. In Southern Hungary and Slavonia inhumations also occur, and in the extreme north-east the latter rite was alone practised.

The tombs are poorly furnished with bronzes, but these conform to the Middle Bronze Age types familiar from the hoards. A wealth of vases counterbalances this poverty in metal grave goods. The ashes were enclosed in cinerary urns, in the Pannonian group generally great pitchers with trumpet-like necks, tall piriform bodies and one or two handles. The South Hungarian urns belong to the class of two-storied pots (Fig. 22, no. 6). The accessory vases and some urns are elaborately decorated. In the Pannonian group proper wide bands of true fretwork (excised, not stamped) are combined with stab-and-drag lines, uniting impressed concentric circles (Fig. 22, nos. 3, 4). In the more southerly groups fretwork is no longer used, while the incised lines often form running spirals, maeanders or rosettes. In the north-east the main decorative device was the conical wart, applied or pinched up and often surrounded by deep grooves.

Both in Slavonia and Serbia art was also manifested in clay figurines decorated in the same style as the vases. They represent a female personage, wearing a richly embroidered bodice and a flounced skirt and decked with necklaces and pendants. The most famous idol of this class, found at Kličevac in North Serbia, was unfortunately lost during the war. The same region has yielded model thrones, axes and other clay votives.

The vase forms in most cases can be traced back to Early Bronze Age groups. Pannonian jugs and dishes have forerunners at Gáta and Tószeg; the hour-glass mug of Perjámos reappears in the Banat cemeteries. Pannonian ware is decorated in just the same technique as the earlier Slavonian ware. Hence the Hungarian plain cannot have been entirely deserted by the Early Bronze Age population, though some of the original groups had shifted their territories or amalgamated with neighbours.

THE RHÔNE CULTURE

Stray flanged celts and flat daggers of bronze as well as bone copies of common bronze pins have been found in several of the later " Neolithic " lake-villages of Switzerland. It would seem that the pile-dwellers lived on in a stone age throughout the Early Bronze Age and part of the succeeding period. By that time, however, we find in the Rhône valley, but unconnected with the lacustrine settlements, graves furnished with a distinctive series of bronzes. The tombs are either small megalithic kists, containing a number of corpses, or individual graves without any barrow over them. The bronze industry, here represented, is inspired mainly by Bohemian and Hungarian traditions though there are some indications of influence from the Iberian Peninsula. The types, however, developed along quite individual lines. Distinctive are the spatuliform celts and the triangular daggers, often bronze-hilted. Besides pins with rolled or even knot-heads, trefoil and disk forms are characteristic, the latter being doubtless a local creation. So, in addition to simple rod bangles and ingot torques, broad bronze collars were developed in a specialized variant as described on p. 122. No pottery is known from these graves.

The engraved bronzes illustrate a continued development of that system of purely rectilinear decoration that had been almost universal in the Early Bronze Age.

The extent and age of the Rhône culture is not yet exactly determined. It is only mentioned here because, as we shall see, it is a prominent constituent of the oldest culture to which the name Keltic can be applied.

THE MIDDLE BRONZE AGE IN
GREAT BRITAIN

In the British Isles the Middle Bronze Age is merely a continuation of the previous period, lacking the sharp demarcation observed in Italy or Southern Germany. Types distinctive of the period on the continent—early palstaves, ogival daggers, rapiers, socketed spear-heads and button sickles—are found stray or in hoards, particularly in the south; north of the Tay no rapiers have been reported and even early palstaves are rare. Yet there is no doubt that rapiers were actually manufactured in England, since moulds for their production are found there—practically the only known rapier moulds. These universal Middle Bronze Age shapes are associated in hoards with specialized local forms—celts with broad flanges near the butt (Fig. 3, no. 4), tanged chisels, spear-heads with loops (Fig. 10, no. 4), true torques, wide armlets with horizontal ridges and a sort of pin with a gigantic ring-head. Even socketed sickles or double-edged razor blades are exceptionally associated with early palstaves and rapiers.

Nevertheless, save for a few ogival daggers, no distinctively Middle Bronze Age types are found in graves. Yet some of our barrows must obviously be contemporary with our Middle Bronze Age hoards. We therefore assign to this phase cremated interments, accompanied by vessels of Early Bronze Age antecedents whose descendants admittedly belong to the Late Bronze Age. Yet such graves may contain flat triangular daggers, and even stone battle-axes, though not flint daggers.

The pot form, thus marked out as Middle Bronze Age, is the so-called cinerary urn in its earlier versions. It is just an enlargement of the food vessel. The commonest type, originating probably in Southern England, is known as the overhanging-rim urn. It undergoes a regular typological degeneration during the period. The oldest form, which is partly contemporary with the latest beakers, had an inverted conical body distinguished by a definite shoulder from the well-marked concave neck, which is surmounted by a broad overhanging rim or collar (Fig. 24, no. 1). Before the end of the Middle Bronze Age the neck disappears, leaving us with rim and body only (Fig. 24, no. 2). In the Late Bronze Age further decadence produces cordoned and bucket urns in which all that is left is one or two ridges encircling the body to represent the overhang of the original rim or this and also the shoulder below the former neck (Fig. 24, no. 3). A contemporary form, originating in Northern England or Scotland and unknown south of the Thames, is just a magnification of the classical food vessel with grooved shoulder. It is therefore termed an enlarged food vessel.

These large pots are made of very coarse clay and

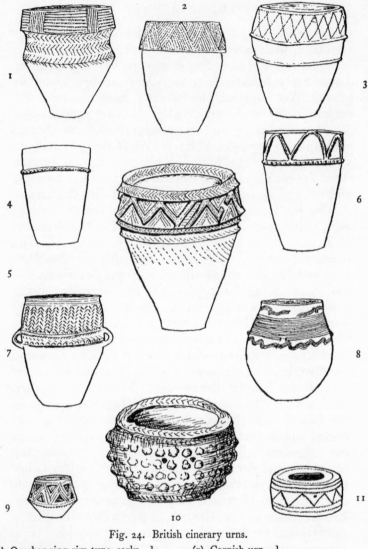

Fig. 24. British cinerary urns.

(1) Overhanging rim type, early. $\frac{1}{12}$
(2) Overhanging rim type, later form. $\frac{1}{12}$
(3) Cordoned urn, Scotland. $\frac{1}{12}$
(4) Bucket urn, Dorset. $\frac{1}{12}$
(5) Encrusted urn, Scotland. $\frac{1}{10}$
(6) Urn of Type 3, group 2. $\frac{1}{12}$
(7) Cornish urn. $\frac{1}{12}$
(8) Globular urn. $\frac{1}{10}$
(9) Incense cup with slits. $\frac{1}{4}$
(10) Incense cup. $\frac{1}{4}$
(11) Grape cup. $\frac{3}{4}$

lack any slip or polish. They are none the less elaborately decorated, principally on the wide collar or the bevelled moulding inside the lip. The ornamentation is executed with a cord, with a chain-looped braid, or by simple incision. The cog-wheel technique and false relief have been abandoned. The patterns are simple zig-zags, triangles, chequers, lattices, and herring-boning.

Contemporary with these urns, often used like them to contain cremated remains and not seldom associated with them in the same grave, go a variety of small vases termed "incense cups" or "pigmy vessels". These are often of much finer clay than the big urns, but seldom approach the delicacy or technical excellence of beaker ware. The decoration includes incised lines combined with dots forming figures such as lozenges. One group of pigmy vessels, sometimes termed "grape cups", are covered with knobby projections (Fig. 24, no. 10). The latter, though quite different from the conical warts of Swabian and Hungarian pottery, recall the ornamentation on a class of Late Neolithic wares from the Danube basin. Another variety of incense cup has triangular slits in the walls, producing a sort of lattice effect (Fig. 24, no. 9). Perforations in the walls are indeed a common feature in the whole class of pigmy vessels.

The funerary pottery and bronzes produce a rather depressing picture of our civilization at this date. That is to some extent offset by the discovery in graves of the period of cups of shale, amber and gold(88) that are, for their age, unique west of the Aegean. The shale and amber cups are simple flat-bottomed vessels with ribbon handles. In shape they recall the wooden cups from Denmark and seem also to have been turned on a pole lathe. Ornamental horizontal grooves may encircle the body, parallel to the rim, and decorate the handle. Five shale and two amber cups are known, all from Southern England, west of Brighton. The gold cup, from a cairn at Rillaton in Cornwall, is of similar shape, hammered out of a single piece of metal and decorated with horizontal corrugations. This group of vessels, unique in North-western Europe, shows that Britain had not lost her originality in the Middle Bronze Age. Moreover, the islands retained their place in European trade. Amber was still imported from Denmark and beads of blue faience came by coastal routes from Crete or Egypt[1]. The most notable of the latter imports are the segmented beads. The type was current in Crete from the end of Middle Minoan times (1600 B.C.), but the trinkets found in Britain are said to resemble rather Egyptian specimens dated to the twelfth century. Similar beads or bone copies thereof have been found in late graves of El Argar type in South-eastern Spain and in megalithic tombs in South-west France and Brittany. Britain's principal export at this period would presumably be tin. But British and Irish gold torques, looped spear-heads and other British types of the Middle Bronze Age reached Northern France in considerable numbers. The spread of the palstave to Western Spain may also be connected with the Atlantic trade from the British Isles.

Dwellings of the period in Britain cannot be distinguished. It is possible, however, that hill camps were already being built. A hoard of rapier blades was, it is reported, unearthed at the bottom of the trench encircling that of Drumcoltram in Dumfriesshire. The fort stands, not on the summit of the hill, but on a spur

[1] Some authorities maintain that many of our vitreous beads were manufactured locally from slag. It remains certain that they imitate Aegean or Egyptian models.

projecting westward from the hill about 675 feet above sea-level. The neck and flanks of the spur are defended by a wide annular moat, 9 feet deep and 30 wide at the brim. The upcast from it has been piled up inside to form a rampart 9 feet high. A causeway 8 feet wide leads across the moat to a gap in the rampart. The fort is a good example of the simpler type widely distributed in the British Isles. The majority at least of the more complex forms belong to the Iron Age.

For the rest, life in prehistoric Britain had undergone no visible change since the Early Bronze Age. Only after the lapse of a considerable interval was our rather sleepy development rudely interrupted by the Late Bronze Age invasion.

Bronze figure
from Sardinia

CHAPTER VI

THE LATE BRONZE AGE

I N contrast to the apparent peace and prosperity of the preceding period, the Late Bronze Age was an epoch of turmoil and migration though it witnessed immense industrial and economic progress, forced upon the barbarians by these times of stress. The growth of population in the tranquil centuries of the Middle Bronze Age among peoples who had not yet settled down to the laborious methods of really sedentary cultivation resulted for the first time in a genuine pressure and congestion on the land. Climatic conditions—intensified drought followed ultimately by a return to moister and colder conditions that favoured the spread of forest at the expense of pastures—may have aggravated the land hunger in individual areas. The cumulative effect of these factors was to produce a bitter struggle for the fertile valleys in Central Europe and the uprooting of small hordes. The regime of bloody tribal wars, later described so grimly in the pages of Tacitus and profitable only to the Roman slave-dealer, had already been inaugurated. The repercussions of the turmoil reached Britain on the one hand and the East Mediterranean coast on the other, there to be complicated by events in Asia that still elude our ken. But the Mycenaean civilization collapsed under barbarian pressure, and northerners overran Anatolia, threatening the Egyptian and Hittite Empires.

These latter disturbances hampered mining and metallurgy in Asia Minor. And Assyrian military requisitions and monopolistic control of ores further restricted the supply. At the same time the state of universal war increased the demand to unprecedented proportions. In continental Europe we witness not only the struggle for land but also one for the control of ores, accompanied by a great intensification of mining activities and the growth of a trade in scrap-metal, marked by the so-called founders' hoards. In Hither Asia the contest for booty was equally accompanied by a quest for new supplies of metal. The merchants and craftsmen of Phoenicia in particular, cut off by barbarian inroads and Assyrian monopolies from local supplies, sought compensations in the West. As at the beginning of the Age of Metals, fresh bands of prospectors sailed from the Eastern Mediterranean, combining kidnapping and piracy with legitimate trade as the *Odyssey* so brightly indicates. Their activities helped to introduce to the western world the secret of the new metal, iron, and a whole series of new types and processes.

Yet the westward tracks of Oriental traders crossed paths already furrowed at an earlier date by pirate galleys from the West Mediterranean isles. The raiders whose descents on the Oriental empires are such a feature of the thirteenth and twelfth centuries before our era may, when finally repulsed, have carried with them westward some of the arts and organization learnt during periods of mercenary service under Hittites and Egyptians. Despite the doubts of eminent Orientalists, the Shardana, Shakalasha and Tursha who harried the confines of Egypt were surely in some sense Sardinians, Sicilians and Etruscans. Whether they hailed in the first instance from Sardinia, Sicily and Italy or only retreated there after failures on the eastern coasts, is far more doubtful(90). Certain it is that the islands and peninsula were the seats of a curious Late Bronze Age civilization which, despite a strong Oriental flavour, was based at least industrially on Central European rather than on Aegean or Asiatic traditions. The peninsula and islands being now incorporated in the continental economic system and having taken over from the Aegean the rôle of mediators in the diffusion of Oriental inventions, a few words on the cultures of Sicily, Sardinia and Italy in the age of transition from bronze to iron will form a necessary prelude to any account of events north of the Alps.

At the same time one general aspect of life in the latter region and also in the East Mediterranean area must be touched upon here; I refer to the spread of cremation cemeteries termed urnfields—a phenomenon already attributed to the Middle Bronze Age in Hungary and Upper Italy, but now becoming general from the Euphrates to the Irish Channel. The bodies of the dead were cremated, their ashes enshrined in cinerary urns and these buried close together with other vessels in extensive cemeteries, termed urnfields. The grave is seldom marked by a barrow; on the other hand cinerary urns were often deposited as secondary interments in earlier barrows. In several parts of Central Europe it was the practice to bore a hole through the walls or base of the cinerary urn. German archaeologists term such an aperture the ghost-hole (*Seelenloch*), believing that it was designed to allow the soul of the departed to escape from the jar that contained his mortal remains.

It should be remembered that cremation was not a new rite, first introduced during the Late Bronze Age. Even in Early Helladic graves on Levkas we find burnt human bones enclosed in large jars. And there are instances of Neolithic cremations from Central Europe, Brittany and England. Isolated instances occur widely during the Early Bronze Age, and the practice was by no means rare in the Tumulus culture of the Middle Bronze Age. To the same period we have assigned a number of barrows covering inurned ashes from the British Isles. Even urnfields may, in Hungary and North Italy, go back to the Middle Bronze Age, but they become general first in the Late Bronze Age or the contemporary Early Iron Age of Greece and Syria.

Conversely it must be insisted that inhumation was not universally abandoned in the latter period. It remained the regular rite in the Illyrian regions, Southern Italy, Sicily and Macedonia till well on in the Iron Age and was still freely practised also west of the Rhine and in parts of Greece. Nowhere, indeed, would burial rite alone constitute a reliable criterion of age. Moreover, in view of the wide distribution of the rite in earlier times, the racial movements inferred simply from the appearance of cremation in Greece and Syria at the beginning of the Early Iron Age (equivalent there to our Late Bronze Age) are very insecurely based.

We begin our account of Late Bronze Age cultures with Italy and the adjacent isles, even though iron was rapidly replacing bronze there; for in the Early Iron Age deposits we find bronze tools of the types still exclusively used north of the Alps, and in the latter regions types of the more southern Iron Age appear in a purely Bronze Age context. Greece on the other hand may still be excluded as having no direct influence on the bronze industry north of the Alps after its very early passage into the Iron Age.

SICILY

During the earlier phases of the Bronze Age, as in the previous Copper Age, the culture of Sicily(44) had maintained an essentially East Mediterranean character. During the first half of Orsi's Siculan II period, which corresponds to our Middle Bronze Age, the native culture had been dominated by Minoan industry and art. Palaces were built with stone foundations as in Greece, and shrines furnished with ritual objects of a Minoan character. The dead were buried in rock-hewn family vaults reminiscent of the usual Mycenaean chamber tombs, though carrying on a tradition rooted in the island since the Copper Age (Orsi's Siculan I). The Siculan II bronzes are inspired directly by Minoan models, though mostly of local manufacture. So we find long rapiers referable to Type II *a* from the Shaft Graves of Mycenae (p. 82) and daggers equally of Minoan ancestry. The common razors (Fig. 12, no. 3), though a specifically Siculan variant, have likewise Cretan prototypes. Fibulae of violin-bow form were worn as east of the Adriatic. And direct imports from Greece were plentiful: the early tombs are furnished with a comparative abundance of Mycenaean (L.M. III) vases and Late Minoan beads were worn.

In the later half of the Siculan II period, represented by cemeteries like Cassibile and Finnochito, farther inland than those described above, the industrial orientation of the island had changed. The dead were indeed still often buried in chamber tombs, a habit which persisted into the full Iron Age or Siculan III. The pottery, too, preserved native traditions enlarged by the inclusion of orientalizing forms such as *askoi*. The safety-pins evolved farther along the separate lines sketched on p. 114. But the remaining bronzes tend to conform more and more to standard types current at the same period in Upper Italy and the Late Bronze Age north of the Alps.

Shaft-hole axes indeed persist in a local form even into Siculan III, but beside them we find in hoards winged celts, socketed celts and lug-adzes. The spear-heads have proper cast sockets and sometimes eyelets in the base of the blade. The commonest razors now conform exactly to the rectangular "Villanovan" type with the handle riveted on (Fig. 12, no. 8) despite some interesting transitional forms with maple leaf blades and flat tangs. This is the period of the serpentine and elbow fibulae (Fig. 14, no. 15) supplemented by simple arcs.

A very similar culture reigned at the same time in Southern Italy, a region that had always been closely allied to Sicily since Neolithic times. One notable type, assignable strictly to the local Iron Age, was a short sword provided with a flange carried right round the flat tang to hold the plates of the hilt and the pommel. The type is directly derived from a familiar L.M. III short sword.

In both regions large founders' hoards(93) attest at once an economic reorganization and social disturbance. Both Oriental and northern elements have been obtruded upon the native culture in a manner not yet plain. At the same time the resultant cultures exerted an influence on the West as the Siculan fibulae from the hoard at Huelva show(92). How the Siculan and South Italian spear-heads with eyelets in the base of the blade are related to the similar and contemporary British type is less clear.

SARDINIA

Far more insular and consequently puzzling is the vigorous civilization that grew up in the great island farther north. Sardinia is rich in copper and silver.

Even during the Copper Age(3) it had been an important centre of population and industry. Elaborate rock-cut tombs, sometimes carved with bulls' protomae and including marble statuettes among their grave goods, disclose Aegean inspiration. On the other hand, numerous bell-beakers and West European daggers are clearly occidental features. A similar blending of Eastern and Western traits characterizes the Late Bronze Age of the island.

Chambered tombs continued to be used as burial places even then, but have for the most part been plundered. The period is better known from dwellings —peculiar round towers termed *nuraghi*. The Sardinian Bronze Age is therefore often alluded to as the nuragic period.

A nuraghe(95) is an approximately conical tower, built without mortar, of rough, almost megalithic blocks. The only external opening was a low, tunnel-like doorway that eventually gave access to a large beehive-chamber. A winding stair in the thickness of the wall led to one or more upper storeys of similar plan. The nuraghi were evidently the castles of martial chieftains. At their feet clustered the round beehive huts of their peasant henchmen. Such strongholds are strung out at relatively short intervals along the valleys or fertile plains, evidently implying a peculiar clan organization in which the need for defence outweighed all other considerations.

In addition to the fortresses a number of partly coeval structures of a sacral character have recently been explored by Prof. Taramelli(97). These generally include subterranean sanctuaries from which numerous votive bronzes may be recovered. That at Santa Anastasia consisted of an outer temple with a façade of dressed stone, from which a flight of steps led down to a circular pit covered with a corbelled roof.

The castles had been long occupied and repeatedly plundered, leaving few relics of their original occupants. A better idea of the bronze industry of the nuragic age may be obtained from numerous hoards(96) that testify in some cases to the piety of the islanders, in others to the disturbed conditions of the times. These depots belong for the most part to a time when iron was already in general use on the Italian mainland, but still contain archaic types, directly descended from quite ancient models and accordingly produced by a school of craftsmen whose divergent specialization must have begun in pure Bronze Age times. Their archaic traditions are rooted mainly in continental workshops. Few industrial types or weapons are East Mediterranean or Asiatic, though eastern influences are conspicuous in the votive bronzes. So, among the axes, curiously splayed flanged celts, two-eared palstaves and two-looped socketed celts were the commonest types current. (The founders' hoards contain also old Copper Age flat celts collected for recasting.) On the other hand, double-axes and axe-adzes might be Aegean types, though the tubular projection that surrounds the shaft-hole is more reminiscent of Hungary. Again the typical weapons are curious bronze-hilted daggers, rather like Early Bronze Age forms, or very archaic triangular or ogival types, swords with pronounced midrib and spur for the hilt or flanged tang. Socketed spear-heads, socketed sickles and rectangular razors, resembling the Villanovan blades but that the handle was cast in one piece with the blade, are also conspicuous. The rather rough pottery includes notably *askoi* and jugs with thrown-back necks and cutaway lips, both old Aegean and Anatolian shapes.

In the nuragic sanctuaries and hoards we find an extraordinary variety of votive statuettes and models in bronze. Figures of warriors, crude and barbaric in execution but full of life, are particularly common. The warrior was armed with a dagger and bow-and-arrows or a sword, covered with a two-horned helmet and protected by a circular buckler. The dress and armament leave no doubt as to the substantial identity of the Sardinian infantryman with the raiders and mercenaries depicted on Egyptian monuments as "Shardana". At the same time numerous votive barques, also of bronze, demonstrate the importance of the sea in Sardinian life.

This extraordinary culture accordingly shows indications of relations with the West—two-eared palstaves, socketed sickles—with Hungary and even perhaps with the Caucasus (statuettes and other models very like the Sardinian have turned up there) in addition to Central Europe and Upper Italy. Amber beads from the nuraghi may even mean connections with the far North. Were the Sardinian smiths originative innovators whose new models were carried westward and imitated there, or merely slaves who copied at the dictation of their pirate masters the odd types the latter picked up in distant raids? And how are the nuraghi related to the Scottish brochs, similar in several architectural details and evidently symptomatic of an analogous clan organization? Above all, were the Sardinians of the Late— nay belated—Bronze Age descendants of the Copper Age population who had seen service under Egyptians and Hittites, or did new arrivals from Asia Minor or the Caucasus dominate these? Such questions inevitably rise only to be dismissed as unsolved.

THE VILLANOVA CULTURE IN ITALY

While Sicily, South Italy and Sardinia were new and by no means secure acquisitions of the continental economic province, it had included Upper Italy since the beginning of the Bronze Age. There, as noted in the last chapter, the dominant cultural group during the Middle Bronze Age was that of the *terremaricoli* who even penetrated to the extreme South as well. A later phase in the same people's culture is illustrated by the urnfields of Bismantova and Fontanella south of the Po, of Pianello in the Marche (East Central Italy) and Timmari in Apulia.

These cemeteries are marked as later than the typical *terremare* by the types of razor, safety-pin and bracelet. The razor has a quadrangular blade with separate handle riveted on (Fig. 12, no. 8). In addition to violin-bow fibulae, generally with beads on, and sometimes with figure 8 twists in (after the style of Fig. 14, no. 14), the bow, simple arched bows and others with two loops were current. Ingot torques with twisted wire bodies and wire finger-rings with spiral ends were also worn. The distinctive pot form is already a storeyed or biconical urn. Such consist of a base in the form of an inverted conical bowl with inturned rim surmounted by a conical neck with everted lip. The parts are separated by a pronounced shoulder rather than a keel. The ornament, restricted to the upper cone, is limited to incised triangles, chevrons, ⊐⌐ or ∞ figures and dimples or warts encircled by grooves (Fig. 25, no. 1). A hoard, of the same date (Randall-MacIver considers it later), indicates that cups of beaten bronze, decorated with embossed knobs, were already in use. These cemeteries may be dated between 1200 and 1050 B.C.

A little later a belt of Italy from the Adige to the Tiber is found to be thickly settled by an industrious folk, termed Villanovans after the suburb of Bologna where their culture was first identified. Pigorini and his disciples hold that they were just the descendants of the *terremaricoli*; they would then be the Umbri and Latini of Roman tradition. Randall-MacIver prefers to invoke a second invasion from an unknown "Hungary" to explain the Villanovans. Assuming the first interpretation to be the more correct, as it is the more economical, we may call the northern Villanovans Umbrians, the southern ones, differentiated from the former by minor peculiarities, Latins. We must note, too, that the Villanovan culture is divided between three chronological phases, termed respectively Benacci I, Benacci II and Arnoaldi after the peasants on whose farms typical cemeteries were dug up. Iron was in use throughout these three periods and the two last are excluded altogether from the purview of this book.

The Villanovans, like their ancestors of the *terremare*, were primarily peasant farmers, living in mean huts grouped in villages of very modest size. The round huts themselves with walls of wattle and daub are represented for us by the models used as ossuaries among the "Latins" (Fig. 25, no. 5); the famous temple of Vesta preserves a glorified version of the same primitive hut.

But these farming communities included skilled metal-workers and traders. Round Bologna vast depots of scrap-metal, the so-called "foundries", have been discovered. Old tools, weapons and ornaments were gathered here for resmelting from every corner of Europe as the types included in the hoards show; even British socketed sickles are represented. In return for

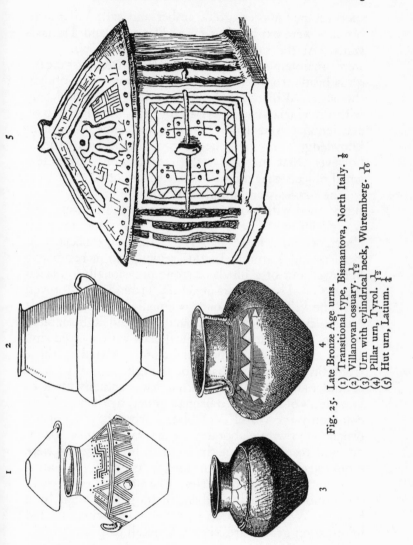

Fig. 25. Late Bronze Age urns.
  (1) Transitional type, Bismantova, North Italy. ⅛
  (2) Villanovan ossuary. 1/12
  (3) Urn with cylindrical neck, Würtemberg. 1/10
  (4) Pillar urn, Tyrol. 1/12
  (5) Hut urn, Latium. ¼

such scrap, for ores, gold, amber and salt, Villanovan bronzes were exported as far as Denmark and Transylvania. At the same time relations, direct or indirect, were maintained with the Eastern Mediterranean; glass beads from Villanovan graves leave no doubt on this score. Villanovan bronze work agrees too closely with Phoenician and Assyrian for the resemblance to be accidental. And from that quarter came eventually knowledge of the new metal, iron. In Benacci I times, however, that material is represented only by a few small objects that might have been imports.

The graves were simply holes in the ground, sometimes lined with stone slabs, in which the cinerary urn was deposited. The ossuary itself was sometimes enclosed within a large jar termed a *dolion*, especially in Etruria and Latium. In this region, too, a receptacle hollowed out of a block of stone occasionally replaced the *dolion*. The *dolion* is generally a rough two-storeyed jar. The Villanovan ossuary is equally two storeyed. It resembles a bowl with inverted rim and a horizontal handle, surmounted by a conical neck with splayed rim. It is, that is, a biconical urn closely related to those from Bismantova or Pianello, though with a broader shoulder (Fig. 25, no. 2). Often it was actually made of two pieces of hammered bronze united by rivets. More commonly the vessel is of black carboniferous pottery ornamented with elaborate maeanders, triangles, lozenges and rosettes. Sometimes small bronze studs were set in the clay to enhance the effect. As noted, the Latins used hut models as ossuaries. The urn was covered in the Umbrian area by a dish, in the Latin often by a helmet. While cremation was the general rite, isolated inhumation graves are known from all districts.

The commonest tools are celts with terminal wings

and very wide blades, knives with a spur-like tang,
quadrangular double-edged razors (Fig. 12, no. 8)
or semilunar single-edged specimens (a later type),
tweezers and fish-hooks. The best known weapon is
the socketed spear-head, but antennae swords (Fig. 8,
no. 11) were imported and presumably used. The head
was protected with ovoid bronze casques, surmounted
by broad, decorated crests. Horses were controlled by
bronze bits, the cheek-pieces in some instances taking
the form of stylized steeds. Among the ornaments may
be mentioned broad girdles of hammered bronze, pins
surmounted by small knobs or terminating in a shepherd's crook, simple arc fibulae and early developments
thereof, massive bracelets with overlapping ends, and
ribbon cylinders. Besides ossuaries, cups and buckets
(situlae) were made of hammered bronze.

Villanovan art is unmistakable. The vases, girdles
and helmets of bronze are decorated with rows of
bosses, beads or concentric rings, all embossed, and
sometimes supplemented by engraved lines that reproduce the patterns known already from the pottery.
A very distinctive and popular motive is moreover a
pair of birds' heads projecting from a circle or wheel
(Fig. 27, no. 3). The design is presumably a solar symbol
connected with the sun disk of the Egyptians probably
through a Hittite or Phoenician variant.

THE LAUSITZ CULTURE

The knowledge of iron-working naturally traversed
the Alps from Italy with a material retardation, so that
even throughout Benacci I times a pure Late Bronze
Age was ruling in Central Europe. Here two or three
great urnfield groups succeed the Early Bronze Age
cultures in the fertile valleys and along the riverine

trade routes while the Tumulus culture persists in the uplands and heaths, modified by these neighbours.

The most conspicuous of the urnfield cultures is known by the name of Lausitz, a part of Saxony and Western Silesia where it is richly represented. It originated there or farther east out of Aunjetitz antecedents, possibly mixed with other undefined ingredients. From this cradle it spread to occupy the whole area from the Saale to the Vistula and from the Spree to the Austrian Danube and the Slovakian mountains.

The Lausitz folk were primarily peasant farmers, but were at pains to control trade routes and supplies of ore. In their communities dwelt competent smiths whose moulds, anvils and founders' hoards have come down to us. The people dwelt probably in log-cabins, built of trunks laid horizontally and supported by posts, quite like the dwellings of American pioneers. The houses were normally long one-roomed halls with the entry on the small side.

The dead were cremated, and their ashes, enclosed in cinerary urns, deposited in extensive cemeteries, sometimes under a barrow. The characteristic Lausitz ossuary is constituted by two truncated cones placed base to base. It was normally covered by a dish and accompanied by a high-handled mug, an amphora and a rough pot. In later graves, vases with side spouts, termed feeding-bowls, vessels in the shape of animals, and clay rattles occur. Apart from the rough pots, Lausitz vases are generally smooth and often burnished. At first they were buff in colour; later dark-faced wares became more popular, and graphite was even used to intensify the effect. The ossuary is normally plain, save for scratches radiating from the base. Other vessels were decorated at first with large conical warts projecting out of a round

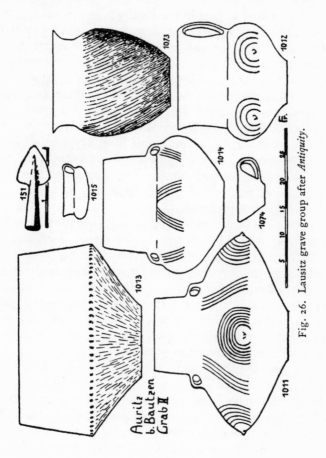

Fig. 26. Lausitz grave group after *Antiquity*.

depression. Later warts gave place to flutings or corrugations, oblique or forming semicircles (Fig. 26).

The Lausitz people used celts with terminal wings and an ear, or a socketed form, knives with a spur for the attachment of the handle or with a metal handle terminating in a ring, button sickles and eventually horse-shoe razors and tweezers. But celts and perforated axes of stone, arrow-heads of flint or bone and many implements of horn and bone were still used. The favourite weapons were spears with lanceolate socketed heads, and arrows, tipped with flint, bone or socketed bronze points, supplemented by comparatively rare swords with flanged tangs. The horse had certainly been domesticated. He was controlled by bits ending in horn cheek-pieces.

Common ornaments in Lausitz graves are pins with a vertically pierced eyelet in a spur projecting from the shaft, massive armlets with overlapping tapering ends, cylinders, ingot torques with twisted body, finger-rings of several coils of wire terminating in spirals, spectacle-spiral pendants and flat buttons with a loop on the back. Safety-pins were rarely worn; all were of the two-member family with a flattened oval bow. Beads of glass or amber are only occasionally found in graves. Gold, on the other hand, chiefly in the form of wire, is not uncommon in Bohemian settlements. The precious metal must have been carried in this form as a medium of exchange, but curious ornaments were made by plaiting gold wire together. Finally in the later phase of the Lausitz culture a few bronze cups of Italian style found their way to Bohemia.

This culture was cradled, as we have indicated, in a southerly corner of the North European plain. Thence it spread over the mountains into Bohemia and across

Moravia into Lower Austria and Slovakia. On the borders of its homeland it grew into the so-called Silesian culture which likewise spread southward and was flourishing in Eastern Bohemia and Moravia when iron was introduced into those regions along the amber trade route from Italy to East Prussia.

In Central Bohemia the Lausitz invaders met the people of the Tumulus culture advancing from the West as well as remnants of the old Aunjetitz population. Under these conditions there arose here in the latest Bronze Age (Kraft E) a specialized group, termed the Knovíz culture, which deserves a brief mention. Besides its urnfield cemeteries we know here deep pits, some perhaps dwellings, others rubbish pits or silos. In the latter we find, together with broken animal bones and other kitchen refuse, human bones, hacked about with knives and split to extract the marrow. Evidently cannibalism was not unknown to this people in Central Europe. Civil servants, engaged in suppressing the practice in Africa or New Guinea, may like to remember that it was current in Europe 3000 years ago, and that among a comparatively advanced group. For the cannibals made splendid pots. Their cinerary urns are based upon a degenerate Lausitz ossuary that has lost its angularity, surmounted by a swelling neck, so as to give the impression of two vases one on the top of the other. Broad-brimmed bowls with twisted pillar-like handles rising from the shoulder also deserve mention.

THE ALPINE URNFIELDS

The Knovíz culture already shows the influence of the South-west Bohemian Tumulus culture which in its turn had been profoundly modified by contact with a second group of urnfields. The latter had developed on the Upper Danube and its tributaries in Austria, Bavaria and the Tyrol, whence it spread down the Rhine and across Switzerland. This Alpine culture is a far less coherent group than the Lausitz; probably it had several roots constituting originally distinct groups, and no doubt it absorbed in its expansion diverse elements. It may have originated among some descendants of Early Bronze Age folk dwelling in the valleys (at Gemeinlebarn in Lower Austria and Straubing in Bavaria both periods are represented in the same cemetery), influenced (whatever that may mean) by Hungarian groups, the Lausitz culture and its neighbours, the tumulus-builders. Lausitz "influence" is certainly patent in the use of typical Lausitz ossuaries in Lower Austria and even far away in the Tyrol. Some indeed would contend that it was constitutive: the whole group would owe its rise and specific character to an actual infusion of Lausitz folk, perhaps as an organizing force bringing together other communities. That certainly is a simple explanation, perhaps too simple.

Yet in its general character the North Alpine culture was very similar to the Lausitz, though richer and more warlike. Its authors dwelt in log-cabins or pit-dwellings. They walled off projecting spurs of the mountains (promontory forts) or defended hill-tops, the walls in each case being of stone and turf, strengthened with a palisade (98). As elsewhere, these fortifications would be places of refuge rather than permanent villages; the latter were probably situated in the valleys. The miners of the Tyrolese copper lodes and the rock-salt of Hallstatt, whose methods have been sketched in an earlier chapter, belonged to our North Alpine group. And the rich cemetery of Hallstatt, that gives its name to the First Iron Age in Central Europe, is an urnfield of the type described below, though of later date. The long timbered galleries, the shafts and ladders and other workings which the visitor to Hallstatt may still admire are apparently pure Bronze Age.

Cremation was of course the normal burial rite, and an urn was deposited in every grave. Sometimes, however, the ashes were laid outside it. The urn itself, often very large, was globular or piriform, but always provided with a cylindrical neck surmounted by a projecting brim (Fig. 25, no. 3). It might serve as a *dolion* containing the ossuary proper, generally a smaller version of the same type. In the Tyrol the ossuaries' rims are supported by twisted pillar-like handles (hence the name "pillar urns"). The walls may be decorated with warts and "false cord impressions" obtained by rolling a twisted ring over the soft clay. With such cylinder-neck urns true Lausitz ossuaries are sometimes encountered as noted above. The accessory vases— jugs, dishes, and cups—are usually fine, often polished with graphite and decorated with incised patterns, flutings, or conical warts.

Typical implements are celts (axes and adzes) with terminal wings and an ear (Fig. 3, no. 8), socketed chisels and gouges, a wide variety of single-bladed knives, grooved sickles, fish-hooks, and razors with an openwork metal handle, at first with an irregular oval blade slit at the end, later horse-shoe shaped (Fig. 12, no. 7). The distinctive weapons are slashing swords with richly engraved bronze hilts or with flanged tangs, giving place later (Kraft E) to Hungarian, Mörigen and antennae types. In addition to swords the warrior used spears with socketed heads, and bronze-tipped arrows.

A wealth of ornaments is found in these graves in contrast to the poor Lausitz interments. The commonest pins have large poppy, vase (Fig. 14, no. 11), turban or bulb heads. Safety-pins of violin-bow type are found sporadically in the Tyrol, and others with a wiry bow twisted in figure 8's and terminating in a horizontal spiral catch-plate, in Bavaria. Massive bracelets decorated with ribs (Fig. 15, no. 1) encircled the arms. The girdle was fastened with disk-shaped clasps. On it or on a necklace were hung pendants in the form of a wheel as well as glass, amber, and gold beads and spectacle-spirals of bronze wire. Gold disks ornamented with rings of stamped circles have been found in some graves and were doubtless solar symbols.

Finally vessels of beaten bronze occur even in the earlier phase (Reinecke and Kraft D). The commonest are cups decorated with embossed circles as in Italy. But a contemporary barrow at Milaveč in Bohemia contained a remarkable bronze bowl, shaped like the usual cinerary urn but mounted on a little wheeled car.

In art a revival of spiral decoration is to be observed on sword hilts of phase D. But even then concentric circles and arcs were commoner, and in phase E these alone survive.

In addition to the solar symbolism of the pendants, curious cult objects now meet us in the settlements. These are made of clay in the form of a pair of horns and very likely served as firedogs, the hearth being of course a place of sanctity. None the less these objects are derived in the last resort from the "Horns of Consecration" that had played a prominent part in Minoan cult from Early Minoan times till the collapse of the Mycenaean culture.

The urnfields just described were in their earlier phases concentrated in the valleys of the Upper Danube, the Inn and the Isar. In the highlands on every side the tumulus-builders lived on still. But they now practised cremation regularly, though seldom, save in Bohemia, enclosing the ashes in cinerary urns. Their pottery was profoundly influenced by that of the urnfields, and most of the bronze types just described might also be found under barrows. The old bronze-studded wooden targe was now at times replaced by a buckler of hammered bronze. Unlike the British products, the Bohemian and South German shields are definitely convex all over and lack any distinct umbo. They were strengthened with concentric ridges hammered up from the inner side and were manipulated by a pair of small handles and one big central handle (Fig. 30).

The North Alpine urnfield culture is of such importance in British archaeology that its development during the last phase of the Bronze Age (Kraft E, Reinecke Hallstatt A) and into the Early Iron Age deserves a rather more detailed examination. Two zones must be distinguished. The inner zone, extending northward to the Main with its core in Switzerland and Bavaria, was nourished by the industry of the lake-dwellings and the trade of the western amber route.

The Bronze Age lake-villages of Switzerland and Upper Bavaria seem to result from the synoecism of older pile-hamlets(100) effected under the leadership of the urnfield folk with the collaboration of the authors of the Rhône culture and perhaps of immigrants from Upper Italy(52). The new pile-villages, situated farther from the present shore than their neolithic forerunners, were regular industrial settlements. Individual villages would even specialize in the manufacture of a particular kind of article—for instance, armlets. Their manufactures were exported to Hungary, Silesia and the North Sea.

In return, Danish bronzes and amber, Hungarian swords, Villanovan horse-trappings and metal vessels flowed in. Stimulated by the blended traditions of their compatriots and by contact with foreign centres of industry, the clever smiths devised original types of tool, weapon and ornament.

Noteworthy among these are knives like Fig. 11, no. 7, antennae and Mörigen swords (Fig. 8, no. 10), horse-shoe razors (Fig. 12, no. 7), pins with hollow globular heads decorated with inlaid eyes, and great hollow bracelets either closed and kidney-shaped (*Nieren-ringe*) or with open splayed-out ends. More generalized types of course occur. While socketed chisels and gouges were quite the rule, winged celts with the wings near the butt and a loop (Fig. 3, no. 8) were far commoner than socketed celts. Bronze bits (Fig. 13, no. 7) were manu-factured to control the horses though those with horn cheek-pieces remained in use.

The fine black or grey pottery includes most urnfield forms and, in addition, globular vessels with a narrow out-turned rim, and tulip-shaped beakers with an almost pointed base. Fluted decoration, fretwork, as in the Tumulus culture, and very neat engraved patterns, often curvilinear, adorned the vases. A rare technique was to inlay the depression of the fretwork with tin. The latest vases show the polychrome decoration of Hallstatt types —stripes blackened with graphite on a ferruginous red wash.

The art of the lake-dwellings[52] is characterized above all by the minute exactness with which the linear patterns were executed. The patterns themselves include circles and semicircles but no spirals. Some pots, how-ever, exhibit a sort of maeander in which the angles have been rounded off. In this connection we may note, too, rattles of animal form and the horn-shaped fire-dogs already described.

The civilization of the lake-dwellings in Bavaria, Switzerland and Savoy, begun already in Reinecke's phase D of the Bronze Age, reached its zenith in the succeeding phase but lasted into the Early Iron Age (Reinecke's Hallstatt B). In that period invaders sacked the villages, while a recurrence of moister climatic conditions led to their final desertion. But by that time urnfield folk, whose funerary pottery shows them to be directly descended from the lake-dwellers, were settling in Northern Spain.

The urnfield people from the Danube basin occupied the valleys of the Rhine, the Neckar and the Main, bringing in their train Swiss and Bavarian elements and absorbing others from the native Tumulus groups. Thus we find inhumations as well as cremations. Throughout this area the essential features of the urnfield culture in its later phase were well maintained, and Swiss bronzes circulated freely. But directly we cross the Main or the Saône we enter impoverished provincial regions where archaic urnfield types persisted in a context that transcends the limits of the pure Bronze Age. The urn-field folk spread, that is, both into Holland and Central France, but lost touch with the creative centre and became economically isolated.

We have already described the gradual spread of the Tumulus culture across Central France. Particularly in Aube we have many burials of this class assignable to phase D(4). But the tumulus-builders were followed by urnfield folk. A cemetery of this type, discovered at Pouges-les-Eaux, Nièvre(102), is the best available evidence of this, though many sherds labelled "âge du bronze" in French museums indicate a wider distribution for the culture. At Pouges, as on the Rhine, inhumations occurred side by side with cremations. The bronzes included two razors, one with openwork handle of the type current on the Upper Danube in phase D, the other flat-tanged like some Sicilian and all British blades (Fig. 12, no. 10). The pots on the contrary look rather like degenerate versions of the types current in Switzerland during phase E (Hallstatt A), to which also most of the pins could be assigned. It looks almost as if a band of urnfield folk had clung tenaciously to some types current in their homeland at the time of their departure while adopting contemporary models in other directions. At the same time the hoards (101) suggest that South-eastern France was winning a certain independence of Central European traditions and was susceptible to currents coming, not from the Danube or Upper Italy, but from Sardinia and Sicily.

The phenomena observed on the Lower Rhine in Belgium and Holland in other respects reproduce those noticed in France. The urnfield folk spread thither slowly and mixed with tumulus-builders. Urnfield types of vases, all very degenerate, persisted well into the Hallstatt period. Scarcely any bronzes are found in graves, and hoards are inordinately rare. Still razors of archaic form occur as in France.

THE LATE BRONZE AGE IN THE NORTH

The Teutonic craftsmen in Denmark, Sweden and North Germany maintained the high standard of skill achieved during the Middle Bronze Age. The austere beauty of the earlier art was, however, sacrificed in the more florid products of the later. In general, Teutonic culture in the Late Bronze Age is only a richer autonomous development of that described in the last chapter. Foreign influences were certainly absorbed, but without causing any interruption in the tradition. The most radical was seen in burial rites. Cremation rapidly replaced inhumation. But even this change was by no means catastrophic. During the first half of the Late Bronze Age a barrow was still regularly erected over the remains. The ashes were frequently deposited in hollowed tree-trunks, big enough for a complete skeleton, as in the preceding period. Urn-burial on the contrary was at first exceptional. The rare ossuaries, however, are generally related to the biconical Lausitz type, showing the very strong influence from that culture that reached the Baltic. Another, but certainly native, innovation of the period was to construct round the grave the outline of a ship in stone, a practice that clearly antici-pates the burial rites of Viking times (103).

The Late Bronze Age of Scandinavia falls quite easily into three phases, corresponding to Montelius' Periods III, IV and V. The regular interchange of products with the south makes it clear that these are parallel to Rei-necke's Bronze D and Hallstatt A and B–C respectively. The last phase of the Teutonic Bronze Age is therefore contemporary with the full Iron Age in Southern Germany and the Danube basin. North-eastern Ger-many was becoming increasingly important during the later phases, but during Montelius' V Teutonic culture was also spreading westward to the Upper Rhine and the Dutch coasts. Eventually, however, the brilliant native development was arrested with the political and industrial expansion of the Kelts late in the Iron Age.

A few characteristic Teutonic products may now be briefly mentioned. Socketed celts were regularly used throughout the age. At first they exhibited a ridge in relief down the middle of either face reminiscent of the projecting ends of the split knee-shaft between the flanges of the Middle Bronze Age celt, but by Period IV this motive had become purely conventional. At the same time winged celts, like those of the North Alpine area, were imported. The single-edged knives were scarcely altered at first, but in Period V, when Swiss and other southern types were imported, the native knife-handles sprouted out into opposed scrolls like the pommels of antennae swords. The horse's head handles of the razors were becoming increasingly conventionalized in Period III and gave way to swans' heads or pairs of spirals in Period IV. To that period, too, belong blades engraved with representations of the "solar barque" (Fig. 12, no. 11).

The sword remained the warrior's principal weapon. In Period III the hilt might still consist of alternate bronze and amber disks, with a flat rhombic pommel; in IV the plated tang predominates; while in V antennae, Mörigen, and true Hallstatt swords were imported or even copied locally.

The contemporary ornaments all grew out of older native types, showing that no material change affected Teutonic dress. The most important pins were of course the two-piece fibulae—in III with large flat spiral coils as catch-plates that were replaced in V by large shield-shaped plates (Fig. 14, no. 17). In the latter period there was a revival of simple pins, those with spiral, sunflower (like Fig. 14, no. 8) or saucer-shaped heads being most popular. Another queer pin, to which Early Iron Age deposits at Aegina and elsewhere in Greece offer parallels, has a dumb-bell head formed by joining two disks by a bar at right angles to the shaft. The handsome bronze collars were still worn by ladies during Montelius' III. In IV and V they were ousted by hooked torques, some genuinely twisted, others with the torsion imitated by cast ridges or engraved lines. In V the direction of the torsion often alternates, one strip being twisted to the right, the next to the left and so on (Fig. 17, no. 6). Some torques are even hinged. Tutuli assumed gigantic proportions. In Period III the central spike had already grown into a veritable pillar surmounted by a knob; by IV the disk may be 7 inches across and the pillar rise $4\frac{1}{2}$ inches from the rim; while in V the ornament looks like a pedestalled goblet 6 inches or more across, richly decorated on its surface and equipped with ingenious devices for attachment on the inside (Fig. 17, no. 5).

Late Bronze Age pottery in the Teutonic province is extremely dull. The only attempt at decoration was to smear over the surface with the fingers or a stiff brush. As already remarked, a biconical ossuary was in use from Periods III to V. In the latter period ossuaries in the form of round huts, much as in Latium, were also being made, particularly in Eastern Germany.

The dullness of the pottery is counterbalanced and explained by a wealth of bronze and gold vessels. Many of the bronze cups, buckets and urns were obviously imported from Italy, exhibiting the distinctive forms and decorative devices of the Villanovan bronze industry. But another group of vessels is no less of clearly native manufacture. Among these are the so-called hanging basins of bronze (they may really be grotesquely enlarged tutuli) of Periods IV–V. They have rounded or conical bases, a narrow almost horizontal shoulder and a short vertical neck from which grow two low handles (Fig. 17, no. 4). The base and neck are richly engraved. No less remarkable is the great group of gold vessels, perhaps mainly ritual, assigned to Period IV. They are ornamented with zones of repoussé concentric circles separated by ribbed ridges. In the case of round-bottomed vessels the circles may form a star radiating from the base, or such a star may be left reserved, the space between the points being filled with bosses or circles. The commonest form is a round-bottomed cup without handles. Two remarkable gold vases in the form of a very high-crowned hat, though found respectively in the Rhenish Palatinate and in Central France, seem in style to belong to the Teutonic group.

The gold of these vessels is so thin that many believe them to have been used in ritual only. A number come from bogs where they might have been cast as offerings to some chthonic divinity. And we certainly possess ritual objects of the Late Bronze Age that must have been disposed of in that way, a usage indicated much later in the Norse sagas. The most famous and unambiguous is a bronze horse on wheels[2] connected with a gold-plated[1] disk also on wheels. The disk is 6 inches in diameter. The whole object stands for the solar chariot; after use in some pagan ceremony it had been ritually slain (broken) and cast into the moss of Trundholm in Zealand. The same order of ideas doubtless sanctified some little gold boats found in another Danish bog. The wheeled bowls of Sweden and Mecklenburg, like that from Milaveč in Bohemia, may equally rank as ritual vessels. The boat symbol, combined often with swans' heads, recurs again engraved on razorblades.

The art of the Late Bronze Age is on the whole inferior to that of the preceding epoch. The spiral survives on collars of Period III and grows into a variety

[1] Not of course by electrolysis, but by coating with gold foil.

of scroll patterns in V (Fig. 17, nos. 4, 5). But the purely geometric principle was being already abandoned, the scrolls blossoming out into stylized animals' heads. To the same period belong undoubtedly some of the rock-carvings and ornamented tombs. Even the Kivik grave is assigned by some authorities to the Late rather than the Middle Bronze Age.

In this connection we may refer to the so-called *lurer*, musical instruments indirectly related to the trumpets depicted on the Kivik monument. Some thirty of these instruments have been found, generally in Scandinavia and North Germany, all belonging it seems to Periods III–V. They consist of composite bronze tubes with a total length of as much as 5 feet, but wound in a curious S form. The sectional tubes of which they are composed have been cleverly united either by casting on or sweating on or by elaborate interlocking joints. The lurer each had a range of eight notes and are generally found in pairs, each tuned to a different pitch (Fig. 29).

HUNGARY AND RUSSIA

The Late Bronze Age on the Middle Danube is particularly complicated owing to extensive tribal move-ments. West of the river in Styria, Carinthia and Slovenia, iron came into use very early among Bronze Age groups of indeterminate antecedents, some showing relations with the Hungarian and North Alpine urn-field folks, others with tumulus-builders. In the moun-tains of Bosnia groups of barrows, covering inhumation interments accompanied by bracelets, pins and tutuli characteristic of the (northern) Tumulus culture together with a few fibulae of Adriatic form, constitute the nuclei of the well-known Iron Age cemeteries of Glasinac.

East of the Danube, on the other hand, a belated Bronze Age continued till iron was introduced by bands of Scyths pushing westward across South Russia towards 500 B.C., and by Kelts advancing in the opposite direction rather later.

The Late Bronze Age throughout the region was ushered in by an invasion of people related to the Lausitz and Knovíz groups who settled especially round the copper-bearing regions of Northern Hungary and Slovakia(41). Their distinctive pottery, fluted like the later Lausitz vases, enables us to trace them farther south and indeed right across the Balkans into Macedonia; there they put an end to the Late Mycenaean colonies as indicated in Chapter 1. Everywhere they introduced the socketed celt, swords with plated hilts, and spearheads with lanceolate blades. In North Hungary the socketed celt almost completely displaced the practical shaft-hole axe that had previously been manufactured in the regions. In Transylvania, however, elaborate derivatives of the old types were still made.

In Northern Hungary the fusion of the invaders with older inhabitants produced a very flourishing culture. It is illustrated by extensive urnfields, remains of regular industrial villages and rich traders' hoards and "foundries". Among distinctive local types are slashing swords with rich spiral ornamentation engraved on the bronze hilts, and a variety of elaborate fibulae with big spiral catch-plates. An exceptional number of bronze buckets and cauldrons (Fig. 27, nos. 2, 3) and cups of gold or bronze have been discovered in this area, principally on its fringe on the plains of the Upper Tisza. That was evidently a dangerous tract on a great trade route leading from the head of the Adriatic diagonally across Hungary to the Upper Tisza and so to the gold,

Fig. 27.   Bronze vessels.
(1) Gold cup from hoard of Unter-Glauheim, Bavaria. ¼
(2) Bronze cauldron with T handles, same hoard. ⅛
(3) Bronze bucket with birds' heads, same hoard. ⅐
(4) Bronze cauldron, West Scotland (after Anderson). ⅙

copper and salt deposits of Transylvania. The metal
vessels are all of forms current in Italy and decorated
with repoussé bosses in Villanovan style; the buckets
even show the bird's head and circle motive in its
classical North Italian form. Yet the exceptional number
of the metal vessels and the use of presumably native
gold in the manufacture of many suggest that some
at least must be local products. Their distribution
elsewhere, too, is not very different from that of the
undoubtedly Hungarian swords just described.

Between the ninth and seventh centuries, too, South
Russia at last entered the orbit of the European economic
and industrial system for a short time. Particularly in
the Ukraine(105) a local bronze industry arose, inspired
mainly by Hungarian and Central European models.
But here the western types subsist side by side with
developments of native "Copper Age" forms. Thus
socketed celts are found together with peculiar flat celts.
Out of this mixture some interesting varieties were
evolved. We may mention a socketed celt with two
ears, a type which spread across Eastern Russia to the
head-waters of the Jenessei in Siberia(106), and socketed
spear-heads with big semicircular slits in the blades that
must be related to contemporary British types. In the
Ukraine they must be pre-Scythian (seventh to fifth
centuries or earlier); farther north they belong to the
local Iron Age. Yet side by side with these we have
tanged spear-heads of Asiatic ancestry and others with
folded socket as in Crete. To the same period belong the
sickles with a hooked tang.

GREAT BRITAIN

We have already seen that Urnfield cultures, more or
less, connected with the North Alpine group were

spreading in a westerly direction across Central France from Switzerland or the Upper Rhine and down the Rhine into Belgium and Holland. The latter current was further reinforced by one originating in northern Central Germany. Ultimately these movements impinged upon the coasts of Britain and represent the so-called invasion with which our Late Bronze Age may be said to open(107). Actually this "invasion" was a complex process effected by the infiltration of discrete bands of invaders(76)—in this probably resembling the earlier phases of the "Anglo-Saxon Conquest". No doubt the invaders started from various centres and landed at diverse points along our coasts. Some certainly followed the precedent of the Beaker folk and crossed the North Sea from the Low Countries. Others may have come across France to the Channel ports, and a group that appears in Cornwall and Devon had Armorican affinities. The cumulative result was that "Lowland England" was dominated by the invaders, while in the highland country to the north and west the intrusive culture was absorbed in strict conformity with the principle recently enunciated by Fox(71). In the south therefore exotic ceramic types were extensively manufactured, while to the north the Late Bronze Age pottery is directly descended from Middle Bronze Age wares. Nevertheless the changes in economic arrangements and burial rites, presumably introduced by the invaders, affected every part of the island, and their new tools and weapons were distributed evenly throughout the land. Conversely, even in Southern England the native tradition in pottery and bronze work was never entirely interrupted.

Hence in general the invasions produced no radical or abrupt change in economy and industry. Probably the communities, in the lowlands especially, were larger, more agricultural and more settled than before. In Southern England a number of roughly rectangular earthworks defended by ditch and bank(109) can safely be assigned to this period and give evidence of more or less permanent settlement. In this area the people lived in pit-dwellings excavated in the chalk. Air photographs, supplemented by excavation, have also demonstrated that some of the old cultivations known as "Keltic fields" likewise date from the Late Bronze Age(108). Broad rectangular fields, varying in size from 100 sq. feet to 400 by 150 sq. feet, were cultivated with the aid of a foot-plough (such as was recently used in the Hebrides) or a primitive plough drawn by two oxen that did not undercut the sods, on the slopes of the open downs and uplands. Between each field narrow strips were left uncultivated(80). Owing to the slope of the land, soil was washed down from the upper edge of the field and gradually accumulated in a little straight bank against the uncultivated strip at its bottom. The low ridge thus formed is known as a (positive) lynchet, and it is a study of the relation of such lynchets to earthworks of the Late Bronze Age that enables us to date the cultivations. The formation of a lynchet clearly implies a considerable period of cultivation, confirming the impression of sedentary life produced by the settlements. In upland Britain, moreover, a number of very substantial round huts of stone, on Dartmoor and in Anglesey for instance, certainly go back at least to the Late Bronze Age, carrying on an early native architectural tradition. Even villages with elaborate stone defences, like Grimspound on Dartmoor, may be Late Bronze Age(78). Both these solid huts and the fine stone defences are incompatible with a semi-nomadic life, though not implying necessarily that extreme fixity attained by our peasantry since the Saxon conquest.

More permanent occupation is likewise indicated by the adoption of burial in urnfields in place of, or besides, in small groups of barrows. Urnfields comparable to those of the Lausitz folk or the Italici are in fact distinctive of the Late Bronze Age not only in Southern England but even in the lowlands of Scotland as far north as Aberdeen. Very often, however, an old barrow was used for secondary interments in the Late Bronze Age, a practice also noticed in Holland and Scandinavia.

A change in the economic organization of Great Britain is denoted by the "founders' hoards" that appear for the first time in this period(55). They imply a new class of travelling smiths, agents or pupils of the great founders of Bologna. Exotic types whose previous history is to be sought in Central Europe, such as winged and socketed celts, leaf-shaped swords with plated hilts, and bugle-shaped objects from harness (107), are specially common in these hoards and again illustrate foreign traditions as well as actual imports. Trade relations with the lands beyond the Channel and the North Sea had naturally been cemented by the movements of peoples from those quarters. But the old traffic along the sea routes to Spain and the Western Mediterranean was revived at the same time, and Britain thus participated in the intensified maritime trade of the Mediterranean basin suggested at the beginning of the chapter. A spear-head of British type (almost identical with Fig. 10, no. 6) was included in a "hoard" dredged up from the harbour of Huelva in Southern Spain(92), and socketed sickles occur even in Sardinia. At the same time, as in the later Stone Age, the maritime trade route was continued round the west coasts of

Scotland presumably to Scandinavia. It is marked by a series of late hoards on Islay, Skye, the Hebrides and Orkney(60). By this route presumably Scandinavian types, such as the sunflower pin, reached Ireland and England.

The British bronze industry of this period is represented only by hoards and isolated objects. Except for razors and a few ornaments, no metal objects are found in the graves. For axe-heads the later palstaves with no indication of flanges below the stop-ridge remained in use side by side with socketed celts and rare winged celts with high-placed wings and an ear. Numerous wood-workers' tools testify to the revival of carpentry, of whose products unhappily no remains survive. To this class belong the socketed gouges, tanged chisels and curved knives (Fig. 11, no. 10). Socketed chisels and socketed hammers probably belong rather to the equipment of the metal-worker. Original products of the native industry are the socketed sickles and socketed double-edged knives (Fig. 11, no. 9). This is also the great age of the bifid razors (Fig. 12, no. 10). Such are found even in graves and settlements.

The slashing sword now became the warrior's principal weapon. Most have flanged tangs originally plated with horn or wood, straight shoulders and a blunted strip (*ricasso*) ending in a nick at the base of each edge. A few are of true Hallstatt pattern, widened out for the pommel like Fig. 8, no. 12. Bronze-hilted swords are rare. Apart from an antennae sword found at Lincoln(2) these bear little resemblance to Central European models, but find rather distant parallels in Sweden. The wooden sheaths that held these swords normally terminated in long narrow chapes (Fig. 9, no. 2). Some, however, were fitted with true winged chapes of Hallstatt form

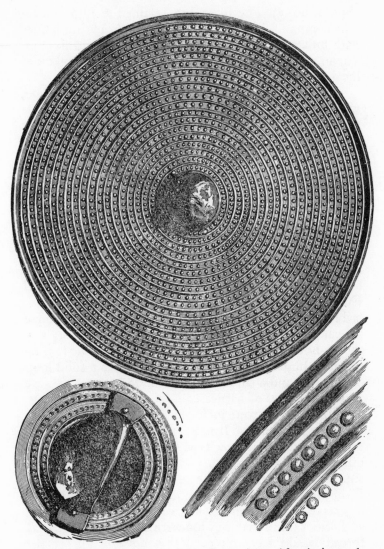

Fig. 28. Bronze shield, Scotland, Late Bronze Age.   After Anderson. $\frac{1}{6}$

(Fig. 9, no. 3). The spear, too, retained its importance. The commonest type has a leaf-shaped head, but blades with lunate openings on either side of the midrib (Fig. 10, no. 6) are native British products derived from older local models.

The warrior was now defended, as in Central Europe, with a round buckler of bronze. The commonest native type exhibits a hollow central boss or umbo encircled by concentric ridges alternating with rings of small bosses. A flat strip of metal, doubled over at the edges, was riveted across the umbo to form a handle (Fig. 28).

Though no wheeled vehicles have come down to us, such were certainly in use. Indeed one domestic hoard, found in the cave of Heathery Burn (Durham)(2), included six bronze cylinders with an internal diameter of 4 inches which are supposed to be nave collars. The horses which drew the vehicle were controlled by bits terminating in antler cheek-pieces just like Central European specimens. A remarkable gold peytrel (collar or brunt) found at Mold (Flintshire)(2), if really Bronze Age at all—and its decoration is of Bronze Age style— shows how richly steeds might be caparisoned. The so-called bugle-shaped objects—tubes with a solid loop on one side and a slit on the other (Fig. 13, no. 5)—are probably pieces of harness.

No safety-pins were included among the toilet articles of a Late Bronze Age Briton. Even pins were still rare, except for the sunflower type (Fig. 14, no. 8). On the other hand, bronze buttons with a loop at the back now supplement the buttons of jet or amber as dress-fasteners. From Ireland come a number of small penannular objects of gold terminating in great cup-like disks. Some authorities think that they too were dress-fasteners(2). A thread would have replaced the movable pin of the contemporary Teutonic fibulae to which the Irish ornaments in other respects bear a very striking resemblance (Fig. 17, no. 8). Other gold objects of similar forms but with a larger hoop might be worn as bracelets (Fig. 15, no. 2). Sir John Evans(5) pointed out the extraordinary resemblance these bear to the so-called *manillas*—the ring money still current in West Africa in his day. It may then be that these Irish gold objects were really currency. The use of identically shaped "money" in West Africa would be a survival from prehistoric times commemorating our Bronze Age trade along the Atlantic coasts.

Gold torques also continued in use as did probably the segmented, quoit-shaped and star-shaped beads of faience, and others of amber and jet. In late Scottish hoards(60) we find beads of blue glass with yellow or white inlays such as would be more at home in the Second Iron Age or La Tène period.

Buckets and cauldrons of hammered bronze are included in several hoards, and, judging by the Heathery Burn cave(2), were in regular use for domestic purposes by well-to-do families. The buckets are of Italian pattern and may well be imported thence. Their models in any case are not older than Benacci II times. The bottom on some British specimens has been strengthened externally by the attachment of a cruciform framework. The cauldrons, on the other hand, are purely British though late in date and probably inspired in the last resort by Italian models. The majority come from Scotland and Ireland, and some are actually associated with iron weapons. They are globular in shape and consist of several bronze plates riveted together and hammered over a hoop that gave stability to the mouth. The elaborate attachments for the loose ring handles have been cast on (Fig. 27, no. 4). The great hoard of bronzes from Dowris in County Meath and that from Duddingston Loch, Edinburgh, were probably contained in such cauldrons.

The Dowris hoard contained also trumpets of types found elsewhere in Great Britain and Ireland. All are much shorter than the Teutonic lurer and lack their distinctive twists. The Dowris types were cast in one piece; some have the mouthpiece at the end, others at the side. A third variety, formed of sheet metal bent over and riveted to form a tube, may date from the Iron Age. In the Irish trumpets, as in the Teutonic lurer, the derivation from an original animal's-horn instrument is patent (Fig. 31).

The best known pottery of the Late Bronze Age is sepulchral and consists of cinerary urns. These naturally fall into two main classes—those derived from old native forms and those inspired by exotic traditions.

The degeneration of the overhanging-rim urn produced, as we saw in Chapter vi, the cordoned or hooped type (Fig. 24, no. 3). In it one ridge of pinched-up clay represents the lower edge of the rim and another below it the old line of the shoulder. This type is commonest north of the Thames, in Wales and in Ireland. Dr Clay(110) believes that in the south of England a similar process led to the formation of what Abercromby calls the Deverel group 2. The urn of this group is cylindrical or bucket-shaped and has a single moulding encircling the body a couple of inches below the lip (Fig. 24, no. 4). This moulding can be treated as a survival of the original overhanging rim. It is, however, generally decorated with finger-tip impressions, a technique which at once relates it to certain foreign types of urn with which the Deverel group 2 is often

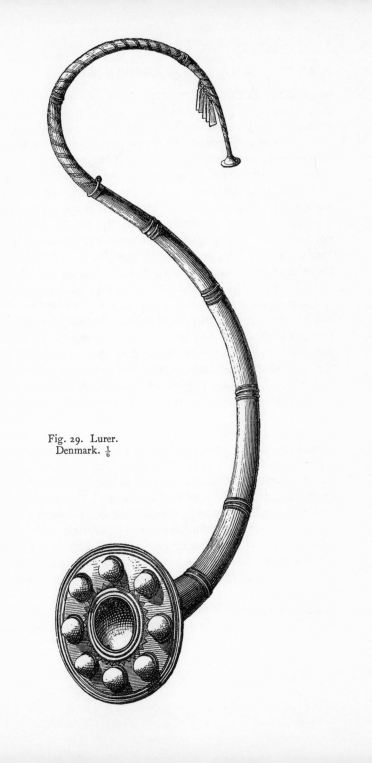

Fig. 29. Lurer.
Denmark. $\frac{1}{6}$

associated. A third native type of urn is that termed by Abercromby "Encrusted". It develops out of the enlarged food vessel in Northern England and Southern Scotland and spreads thence to Wales and Ireland(112). These urns were decorated by applying round pellets or strips of clay to the surface while the vessel was drying and arranging them to form simple patterns—chevrons, squares, concentric arcs or interlaced mouldings. The applied clay was carefully joined up to the body by rubbing with a wet finger, but none the less the strips easily fall off. The strips and even the spaces between them are often incised with a bone point, but never exhibit finger-tip impressions (Fig. 24, no. 5).

Over against these native types, which except for the bucket urns all belong to highland Britain, stands the foreign pottery of invaders as represented in Southern England including Cornwall. The most striking are the globular urns constituting Abercromby's Deverel group 1. The body is globular with four little handles on the line of greatest swell. There is no clearly marked neck, but where it should be comes the decoration, consisting generally of horizontal flutings, simple horizontal incisions, or bands of wavy lines made with a sort of comb (Fig. 24, no. 8). Abercromby rightly noted the similarity of the fluted decoration to that on the urnfield pottery of Central Europe and France.

Abercromby's Type 3, groups 2 and 3, consist of tall bucket-shaped or cyclindrical urns decorated with horizontal, vertical or zig-zag mouldings. The mouldings are normally embellished with finger-tip impressions and, in group 2, often form loops suggestive of handles (Fig. 24, no. 6). The rim is generally slightly everted in a manner reminiscent of metal vessels. Plastic finger-tip mouldings had been used decoratively along the northern shores of the Mediterranean and in Central Europe from Neolithic times. From Italy to Holland they are quite common in the urnfield period. This feature therefore helps to attach the group in question to continental cultures without giving us any clue as to the exact home of its makers.

The third intrusive ceramic type is commonest in Cornwall. It is a slightly biconical urn, the upper cone being much shorter than the lower. Two or four strap handles sit on the keel. The upper part and shoulder is decorated with vertical or horizontal zig-zags, sometimes formed by the impression of a cord (Fig. 24, no. 7). The patterns are thus very similar to those of the Middle Bronze Age overhanging rim urns. But the forms of our group are undoubtedly strongly reminiscent of the Armorican urns of an earlier date described in Chapter v.

One peculiar feature is common to all the three classes of intrusive pottery. On the base of the urn there is often a cross or star in relief on the inside. It has been suggested that these relief patterns were really structural and served to strengthen the base. They would actually be useful if the pot was used for boiling water by dropping in hot stones, and several of the decorated pots came from settlements. Another possibility is that the ridges imitate the stays used to strengthen metal buckets, but these were generally affixed to the outside. Dr Clay regards the crosses and stars as religious symbols. Indeed in some Hungarian urnfields a swastika has been observed in relief inside urns.

A word must be said in conclusion as to the duration of the Late Bronze Age in the British Isles. Quite obviously it everywhere overlaps the Central European Hallstatt period very considerably; the Hallstatt types from our hoards suffice to prove that. Moreover, until recently no connected settlements or cemeteries other than those of the Late Bronze Age were known that could be assigned to the First Iron Age. It was only in the Second or La Tène period that new groups could be identified. In the last few years it has been proved that people with a very late Hallstatt culture, including distinctive pottery, did settle on our shores notably at Park Brow(113) near Cissbury in Sussex, at All Cannings Cross(111) near Devizes in Wiltshire and at Scarborough. But though these new-comers did use pottery of Hallstatt character, their safety-pins were already of La Tène type, i.e., though they brought a culture of Hallstatt ancestry, they and it only arrived in La Tène times so that their coming need not be anterior to 450 B.C. Moreover, the intrusive wares at All Cannings and elsewhere are associated with Bronze Age urn types(110) so that even in Southern England the survival of our Bronze Age culture throughout the whole of the Hallstatt period of Central Europe seems indisputable. In more inaccessible regions it lasted longer still. That is implied in the late associations of the Irish and Scottish cauldrons. The glass beads from the hoard of bronzes on Lewis and from a cordoned urn at Edderton, Ross-shire, both point to a survival well into the Second Iron Age. And in one urn of Bronze Age fabric from Cornwall Roman coins of the fourth century A.D. have been recorded! On the whole, then, the Bronze Age in Southern England must have lasted till about 400 B.C. and elsewhere till at least 200 B.C., probably to the beginning of our era in Scotland.

The beginning of the Late Bronze Age is less easily determined. The intrusive types with which it opens need none of them be later than Reinecke's Hallstatt A. But if they reached here not by trade but as the results of ethnic movement, they might have been already out of date on the Danube before they reached the Thames, just as our Hallstatt pottery would have been already superseded by La Tène wares on the Rhine before it was used at All Cannings.   On the contrary, the Sicilian safety-pins associated with the British spear-head at Huelva imply that such Late Bronze Age types were current here before 900 B.C. So perhaps a date of about 1000 for the first invasions would not be much too high.

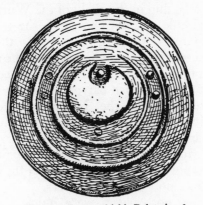

Fig. 30. Bronze shield, Bohemia. $\frac{1}{12}$

CHAPTER VII

RACES

IN the last three chapters we have given a rather cursory account of the culture of the principal communities living north of the Alps between 2000 and 500 B.C. The description of our ancestors' life in Britain towards the latter date is rather an anti-climax after the brilliant civilizations of Sumer, Egypt and Crete with which we started. It is salutary, if depressing, to compare the hovels, dug in the chalk of the Wiltshire downs or built of rubble on Dartmoor, with the great cities of Kish and Harappa that are already two thousand five hundred years older. A single tomb on the acropolis of Mycenae contained more gold than has been collected from thousands of British barrows ranging over fifteen hundred years. And the Mycenaean tombs were poverty-stricken in comparison with the Royal Graves of Ur that are fifteen hundred years earlier. A Middle Minoan II rapier is a foot longer than the finest bronze blade forged north of the Alps. And yet the Bronze Age barbarians had no lack of armourers.

In fact, the northerners were quick to learn and adapt to their peculiar needs those discoveries of the Ancient East that appealed to barbarian requirements. But the techniques and models were in every case supplied by Sumerians, Egyptians, or Minoans. In our period it is not possible to point to a single vital contribution to material culture originating in Europe outside the Aegean area.

And, if it be argued that this poverty in material culture was counterbalanced by an inherent spiritual superiority, we can point to the cannibal feasts of the Knovíz peoples and the human sacrifices depicted on the Kivik tombstone. Certainly Bronze Age burials suggest a monogamous family and a high status for women. But, after all, few Orientals could actually afford a harem, and the queens of Egypt were buried with sufficient pomp. It would be just silly to say that Scandinavian decorative art was superior to Babylonian or Minoan. And no one in their senses will compare the Swedish rock-carvings with even a poor Egyptian bas-relief or the Trondholm horse with a Sumerian bull of 3000 B.C.

No, it is not with their civilized contemporaries in the Eastern Mediterranean that our Bronze Age ancestors must be compared but with the more backward communities of Africa and Malaysia to-day.

Nevertheless the roots of modern European civilization were struck down deep into this unpromising soil. The general economic and social structure that may be inferred from the Late Bronze Age remains persisted with surprisingly superficial modifications throughout the Roman Period in many parts of the Empire. The native houses and fields of Roman Britain did not differ essentially from those of the latest Bronze Age. And after all the direct ancestors of the Romans themselves prior to the rule of the Etruscan kings had been just an Urnfield folk comparable to the inhabitants of the Lausitz and the Alpine slopes. Even in the British Isles many elements of pure Bronze Age culture survived unchanged by subsequent migrations and invasions till late in last century. For example, travellers describe beehive huts of stone and a foot-plough, exactly like those known directly or inferred in Bronze Age Britain, as still current in the Hebrides. Despite the upheavals of the Early Iron Age and the Migration Period one is inclined to believe in a considerable continuity both in blood and tradition between the Bronze Age and the modern populations.

Furthermore, the earliest historical data imply that the principal European nations of antiquity must already have existed, either as distinct peoples or at least as groups in course of formation, before the close of our period. It should, therefore, theoretically, be possible to attach to our main Bronze Age groups ethnic labels, derived from the classical authors. Such an attempt is, however, rendered hazardous in practice both by the extensive and complicated popular movements that took place during the Early Iron Age and also by the ambiguous use of ethnic terms by the Greeks and Romans. It is well to close this book with some account of recent speculations in this direction, but the results up to date are frankly disappointing.

The "ethnic" groups considered in this search almost inevitably become confused with the linguistic groups distinguished by comparative philologists. Language is certainly a cultural, rather than a racial, trait and one of those unifying factors that give to a single people that unity which might find outward expression in a "culture" (as defined on p. 42). The equation of language and culture can, however, only possess a restricted validity. In so far as it is applicable, it gives us a means of supplementing the somewhat vague testimony of ancient writers; for place-names often define very accurately the former distribution of a group or people. A comparison of the distribution of place-names of a given type with that of archaeological remains has yielded good fruit already. This line of research will, I believe, if the complicated problems of the Iron Age are concomitantly unravelled, lead to the ultimate solution of our questions.

It is generally believed that, with the exception of the Mediterranean basin and some corners in the extreme North and West, Europe was occupied by peoples of Indo-European (or Aryan) speech (the great linguistic family to which all modern European languages, except Basque, Magyar, Turkish and Finnish, and also Armenian, Persian and Hindu belong) by the beginning of the Bronze Age. In the Mediterranean basin place-names indicate a much longer survival of a predominantly pre-Aryan population. In the Aegean these would be Leleges and Carians of Anatolian affinities, in Sicily and South Italy, Sicels, and in Spain Iberian tribes whose language survives perhaps as Basque. Beyond the borders of the European economic system to the north-east dwelt perhaps already Lapps and Finns, while it is still open to dispute whether some early peoples in the British Isles, such as the mysterious Picts, belonged to our linguistic ancestry at all. For the rest, Aryan languages must have been in general use. It should therefore be possible to connect the several Bronze Age cultures with branches of the Indo-European linguistic family—the Teutons, Kelts, Italici, Hellenes, Illyrians, Thraco-Phrygians, and Slavs of the philologist.

In the case of the Teutons[1] alone is there any considerable approach to unanimity. The bronze culture of Scandinavia and North Germany is continuous with the demonstrably Teutonic culture of the Roman period. We have even seen that Teutonic cult practices can be traced far back in the local Bronze Age. Though

---

[1] Teutonic is the English term used to denote the whole group of allied languages comprising Anglo-Saxon, Dutch, German, the Scandinavian tongues and ancient Gothic. In Germany the term Germanic is used as by Tacitus. Gothonic has recently been suggested as an alternative by a Dane, Schütte (*Our Forefathers*, Cambridge, 1929).

Scandinavia and North Germany were subjected to
strong "influence" from the Lausitz area in the Late
Bronze Age and even stronger from the Kelts in the
Iron Age, there are no grounds for connecting these
foreign influences with a racial or even linguistic change.
The only serious problem is the attribution of certain
cultures in Eastern Germany which begin in the closing
years of the Bronze Age. Kossinna has dubbed them
"East Germanic", but the researches of one of his pupils,
Petersen, have shown that they disappear from the area
in question altogether before the historical Goths are
traceable there. An identification with the Bastarnae
has been suggested, but rigorous proof is still lacking.

On the origin of the Kelts opinions seem at first
hopelessly divided. The issue is complicated by un-
certainty as to the antiquity and significance to be
attributed to the linguistic division into Brythonic and
Goidelic Kelts. The division rests principally on the
treatment of the Indo-European guttural *qu* which is
represented as a labial, *p*, in Brythonic (e.g. Welsh *pump*
for Latin *quinque*) while it is preserved as a guttural, *c*,
in Goidelic (Gaelic *coic*). Brythonic survives to-day in
Welsh and Cornish and in shepherds' "counts" elsewhere in England, even in Lincolnshire. In Roman
times it was spoken by the Britons and most Gauls. Erse
and Scots Gaelic, introduced presumably by the Scotti
who crossed over from Ireland in post-Roman times,
alone illustrate the Goidelic speech, although there are
traces of the same branch in the Seine valley (32).

It is quite certain that the La Tène culture of the
Second Iron Age (from about 450 B.C.) was created by
Kelts and carried by them to Britain and Ireland and
eastward far across Central Europe. It is less certain
among which group of the Hallstatt period the La Tène

culture arose and whether there were already Kelts
outside the cradle possessing a different culture. On
the second question at least Great Britain and Ireland
might be expected to afford conclusive evidence. Lord
Abercromby boldly suggested that the round-headed
Beaker-folk spoke proto-Keltic, still preserving the *q*
sound, as in Goidelic. That would agree very well with
the views of Professor Kossinna who ascribes the Tumulus culture of South-west Germany, that is clearly
related to that of our round barrows, to Kelts. Unfortunately as far as Britain is concerned there is no
trace of Q-Keltic speech, and Ireland was not reached
by the Beaker-folk. At the same time the recognition of
a quite extensive infiltration in Late Bronze Age times
has greatly complicated the position. If two waves of
Kelts are required in Britain, the Urnfield folk have as
good a claim to be the first as their round-barrow-
building precursors. Correspondingly other Germans
like Dr Rademacher of Cologne have modified Kossinna's theory by making an admixture of Urnfield folk
with the tumulus-builders a condition for their becoming
Kelts proper.

Still more recent researches have resulted in connecting the oldest strata of Keltic place-names in North Spain
with a group of Urnfield folk, culturally descended from
the Late Bronze Age lake-dwellers of Switzerland and
Savoy. It is thus possible to assert with some confidence
that these latter were already Keltic. It is not thereby
determined whether they were the sole Kelts nor what
element in their complex ancestry—Urnfield folk from
the East, authors of Rhône culture and perhaps tumulus-
builders—made their speech Keltic. The association of
Urnfield folk in Britain with the system of agriculture
practised there throughout the Keltic period on the one

hand and the linguistic affinity between Kelts and Italici, who were also Urnfield folk, on the other, would encourage an identification of Kelts and North Alpine Urnfield people. The chief obstacle to such an identification is the desire to connect the North Alpine culture with Illyrians which is mentioned below.

The position of the Italici is less difficult. There are very strong grounds for connecting the *terramaricoli* with the Latini at least, and so with the Romans. Professor Pigorini and his disciples go further, and regard the *terramaricoli* as ancestors also of the Umbrians and Oscans, peoples who like Brythonic Kelts changed Q to P. There is indeed an almost overwhelming case for regarding the Villanovans as Umbrians. And Professors Pigorini and Collini have argued strongly for a derivation of the Villanovans from the *terramaricoli*. Randall-MacIver would, on the other hand, invoke a second invasion from an undefined district in Central Europe to explain the Villanovans—a, to me, gratuitous assumption. But quite apart from this, links between the Oscans and either the Villanovans or *terramaricoli* are not as yet obvious. In particular the Oscans seem to have practised inhumation. Von Duhn therefore has recently propounded a theory of an invasion by "inhuming Italici" who would have occupied both Umbria and the Oscan territory—a theory at the moment very difficult of acceptance. Personally I regard Pigorini's identification of the *terramaricoli* with the ancestors of Latins, Umbrians and Oscans alike as the most economical and plausible theory.

The ancient writers often mention the Illyrians as a great nation occupying the West Balkan highlands and parts of the Danube valley. The modern Albanians are the sole survivors of this linguistic stock. The greater part of the Illyrian territory was occupied until the Roman conquest by tumulus-builders directly descended from the Late Bronze Age group who had settled at Glasinac in Bosnia. A group of tumuli in Southern Italy can equally be identified safely with the Illyrian Iapyges. The tumulus-builders practised inhumation even in the First Iron Age when elsewhere cremation predominated. On the other hand, at the head of the Adriatic the Veneti, who are supposed to be of Illyrian speech, were Urnfield folk. This seems the sole archaeological argument in favour of attributing to the Illyrians the Lausitz and even the North Alpine Urnfield culture —a theory that holds indisputed sway in Germany to-day. From the point of view of toponymy the doctrine is supported especially by the distribution of names containing the allegedly Illyrian word for salt *hal, in places where the Lausitz culture or its influence is discernible—Hallstatt, Hallein, Reichenhall, Halle, Halicz (in Galicia).

Against this it may reasonably be argued that we have in the regions in question during Late Hallstatt times intrusive inhumation graves whose furniture suggests derivation from the south-eastern slopes of the Alps. These inhumationists may have been responsible for the introduction of the Illyrian names in question.

The Thracians have a much stronger claim to the Lausitz culture. Though their centres were in the East Balkans and Hungary, a Thracian or Dacian tribe was to be found on the Lower Vistula as late as A.D. 180 and left perfectly good Dacian place-names in Poland and Silesia. To them at any rate must be ascribed the Pannonian urnfields of the latest Bronze Age in Hungary and Transylvania to which the Lausitz cemeteries are more or less allied. The Late Bronze Age culture of this Tisza district, subsequently overlaid by elements contributed by Scythians and Kelts, seems to be more or less continuous with the historical civilization of the Thracians of Dacia. It was also, earlier at least, connected with the Bronze Age culture of Macedonia and intrusive, perhaps Phrygian, elements in Asia Minor (Troy VII and perhaps earlier) (37). Its attribution to Thracians seems then certain.

As for the Lausitz culture, a third claimant is to be found among the Slavs. The case for a Slavonic attribution of the Lausitz urnfields has been strongly urged recently by several Polish scholars following in the steps of the Czech archaeologist, Pič. The continuity has not, however, yet been entirely demonstrated, and one suspects that political considerations are influencing their championship of this theory as they are the strenuous opposition of all German investigators. Still, otherwise no Slavonic nuclei have been offered us during the Bronze Age.

As for the Hellenes, if they were not already south of the Balkans in pre-Mycenaean times, we cannot identify them to the north. Two northern inroads may indeed have reached Macedonia. The one, marked by fluted ware, started in Hungary but was hardly on a scale to account for the Hellenization of Greece, besides being rather belated for that. The other, bringing inhumation graves, spectacle·brooches, and antennae swords ought on the above view to be connected with Illyrians.

The labelling of Bronze Age groups is accordingly in a very tentative and precarious stage. In most cases a closer analysis of the cultures of the Iron Age is indispensable. We believe that with accurate distribution maps of leading fossils at several periods the question might be solved with almost scientific precision. But

in two key areas, France and Hungary, we are likely to
have to wait long before such maps are available. In
the meanwhile Britain offers a most promising field, and
from a co-operation between archaeology and toponymy
and folk-lore most fruitful results are to be expected.

Fig. 31. Late Bronze Age
trumpet from Scotland
(after Anderson). $\frac{1}{5}$

BIBLIOGRAPHY

ABBREVIATIONS

Antiquity.   *Antiquity*, A quarterly Review of Archaeology, Southampton.

Ant. J.   *Antiquaries' Journal*, Society of Antiquaries of London.

Arch.   *Archaeologia*, Society of Antiquaries of London.

Arch. Camb.   *Archaeologia Cambriensis.*

B.P.   *Bullettino di Paletnologia Italiana*, Parma.

IPEK.   *Jahrbuch für prähistorische und ethnographische Kunst*, Leipzig.

M.A.   *Monumenti Antichi*, R. Accademia dei Lincei, Rome.

Mat.   *Matériaux pour l'histoire primitive de l'homme*, Paris (continued as *L'Anthropologie*).

MSAN.   *Mémoires de la Société des Antiquaires du Nord*, Copenhagen.

PSAS.   *Proceedings of the Society of Antiquaries of Scotland*, Edinburgh.

PZ.   *Prähistorische Zeitschrift*, Berlin.

Real.   Ebert's *Reallexikon der Vorgeschichte*, Berlin, 1924–9.

WAM.   *Wiltshire Archaeological Magazine*, Devizes.

GENERAL WORKS

(1) BURKITT. *Our Early Ancestors.* Cambridge, 1926.
(2) British Museum. *A Guide to the Antiquities of the Bronze Age.* 1920.
(3) CHILDE. *The Dawn of European Civilization.* London, 1924.
(4) DÉCHELETTE. *Manuel d'archéologie préhistorique, celtique et gallo-romaine.* Vol. II. Paris, 1910.
(5) EVANS, JOHN. *Ancient Bronze Implements of Great Britain.* London, 1881.
(6) PETRIE. *Tools and Weapons.* London, 1917.

For CHAPTER I especially

(7) SMITH, SIDNEY. *The Early History of Assyria.* London, 1927.
(8) CHILDE. *The Most Ancient East.* London, 1928.
(9) PETRIE. *Prehistoric Egypt.* London, 1917.
(10) FRANKFORT. *Studies on the Ancient Pottery of the Near East.* Royal Anthropological Institute, Occasional Papers, 6 and 8. London, 1924–6.

(11) WOOLLEY. "Excavations at Ur." *Ant. J.* Oct. 1929.

(12) EVANS, A. J. *The Palace of Minos at Knossos.* London, 1921 ff.

(13) HALL, H. R. *The Civilization of Greece in the Bronze Age.* London, 1928.

(14) BLEGEN. *Korakou,* New York, 1921.

(15) DÖRPFELD. *Alt-Ithaka.* Munich, 1927.

(16) TSOUNTAS. Κυκλαδικα in Ἐφεμερὶς ἀρχαιολογική, 1898–9.

(17) SCHMIDT, H. *Schliemanns Sammlung Trojanischer Altertümer.* K. Museen zu Berlin, 1902.

(18) GJERSTAD. *Studies on Prehistoric Cyprus.* Uppsala, 1926.

CHAPTER II

Mining:

(19) ANDREE. *Bergbau in der Vorzeit.* Leipzig, 1922. (Also article "Bergbau" in *Real.*)

Metallurgy:

(20) GOWLAND. "Early Metallurgy in Europe," *Arch.,* LVI.

(21) LUCAS. "Copper in Ancient Egypt," *J. Eg. Arch.,* XIII.

(22) GÖTZE. "Bronzeguss." *Real.*

Trade routes:

(23) NAVARRO. "Prehistoric Routes between Northern Europe and Italy defined by the Amber Trade." *Geographical Journal,* Dec. 1925.

Climate:

(24) GAMS AND NORDHAGEN. *Postglaziale Klimaänderung...in Mitteleuropa.* Munich, 1923.

(25) WAHLE. "Die Besiedelung Südwestdeutschlands in vorrömischer Zeit." XII. *Bericht der römisch-germanischen Kommission.* Mainz, 1921.

Chariots:

(26) EVANS, A. J. "The Ring of Nestor." *JHS.* XLV.

Potter's wheel:

(27) HARRISON. *Pots and Pans.* London, 1927.

Typological series:

(28) MONTELIUS. *Die ältere Kulturperioden.* I. Stockholm.

Chronology:

(29) MÜLLER, SOPHUS. In *MSAN.* 1914–15.

(30) REINECKE. In *Altertümer unserer heidnischen Vorzeit.* V.

Chapter III

Swords:

(31) Evans, A. J. "The Prehistoric Tombs of Knossos." *Arch.* LIX.
(32) Peake. *The Bronze Age and the Celtic World.* London, 1922.
(33) Parker-Brewis. "The Bronze Sword in Great Britain." *Arch.* LXXIII.

Spear:

(34) Greenwell. "The Origin of the Bronze Spear-head," *Arch.* LXI.

Razor:

(35) Montelius. *Die vorklassische Chronologie Italiens.* Stockholm, 1912.

Fibulae:

(36) Blinkenberg. *Fibules grecques et orientales.* Copenhagen, 1926.
(37) Myres, J. L. *Who were the Greeks?* Berkeley, 1930.
(38) Kossinna. *Die deutsche Vorgeschichte, eine hervorragend nationale Wissenschaft.* 1922.

Pins:

(39) Seger. "Nadel." *Real.*

Jet ornaments:

(40) Callander. "Notice of a Jet Necklace. . . ." *PSAS.* L.

Chapters IV–VI inclusive. Special area

Central Europe:

(41) Childe. *The Danube in Prehistory.* Oxford, 1929.
(42) Behrens. *Bronzezeit Süddeutschlands.* Katalog des römisch-germanischen Centralmuseums, Mainz, 1916.
(43) Kraft. *Die Kultur der Bronzezeit in Süddeutschland.* Tübingen, 1925.

Italy:

(44) Peet. *The Stone and Bronze Ages in Italy and Sicily.* Oxford, 1912.

Spain:

(45) Siret. *Les premiers âges du métal dans la sud-est de l'Espagne.* Brussels, 1889.
(46) —— "L'Espagne préhistorique." *Revue des questions scientifiques,* Brussels, 1893.

(47) Bosch-Gimpera. "Pyrenäen-Halbinsel." *Real.*
(48) Castillo. *La Cultura del Vaso campaniforme.* Barcelona, 1927.
(49) Burkitt. *Prehistory.* Cambridge, 1924.
(50) Obermaier. "Die bronzezeitlichen Felsgravierungen von Nordwestspanien." In *IPEK.* 1925.

Brittany:

(51) du Chatellier. *Les époques préhistoriques et gauloises dans la Finistère.* Rennes, 1907.

Rhône valley:

(52) Kraft. "Die Stellung der Schweiz innerhalb der bronzezeitlichen Kulturgruppen Mitteleuropas." *Anzeiger für schweizerische Altertumskunde,* Zurich, 1927–8.

Great Britain:

(53) Abercromby. *Bronze Age Pottery of Great Britain and Ireland.* Oxford, 1912.
(54) Anderson, Joseph. *Scotland in Pagan Times.* II. Edinburgh, 1886.
(55) Fox. *The Archaeology of the Cambridge Region.* Cambridge, 1923.
(56) Wheeler. *Prehistoric and Roman Wales,* Oxford, 1925.
(57) Coffey. *The Bronze Age in Ireland,* Dublin, 1913.
(58) Macalister. *Ireland in pre-Celtic Times,* Dublin, 1921.
(59) Montelius. In *Arch.* LXI.
(60) Callander. "Scottish Bronze Age Hoards." *PSAS.* LVII.

Chapter IV

Britain:

(70) Fox. "On two Beakers of the Early Bronze Age." *Arch. Camb.* 1926.
(71) —— "A Bronze Age Barrow on Kilpaison Burrows." *Arch. Camb.* 1926.
(72) Crawford. "Barrows." *Antiquity,* I.
(73) Callander. "Recent Archaeological Research in Scotland." *Arch.* LXXVII.
(74) Allcroft. *The Circle and the Cross.* London, 1927.
(75) Stonehenge: Cunnington and Newall, in *WAM.* XLIV; Arbor Low, Gray, in *Arch.* LVIII; Stennis, Thomas, in *Arch.* XXXIV.
(76) Kendrick. *The Druids.* London, 1927.
(77) Coffey. *New Grange.* Dublin, 1912.

(78) Dartmoor Research Committee Reports in *Trans. Devonshire Association*, XXVI–XXVII, XXIX, XXX.

(79) FAIRBAIRN. "Further Discoveries...in Hut-circles...in Ayrshire." *PSAS*. LIV.

(80) CURWEN, C. "Prehistoric Agriculture in Britain." *Antiquity*, I.

CHAPTER V

Scandinavia:

(81) SOPHUS MÜLLER. *Oldtidens Kunst i Danmark*, Copenhagen, 1921.

(82) SOPHUS MÜLLER. *Ordning af Danemarkes Oldsager*. Copenhagen, 1898.

(83) MONTELIUS. *Minnen från vår Forntid*. Stockholm, 1917.

(84) SPLIETH. *Inventar der Bronzealterfunde aus Schleswig-Holstein*. Kiel, 1900.

Germany:

(85) NAUE. *Die Bronzezeit in Oberbayern*. Munich, 1894.

(86) SCHAEFFER. *Les tertres funéraires dans la Forêt de Haguenau*. Haguenau, 1926.

Italy:

(87) MUNRO, ROBERT. *Palaeolithic Man and Terramara Settlements in Europe*. Edinburgh, 1912.

Britain:

(88) NEWALL. "Shale Cups of the Early Bronze Age." *WAM*. LIV.

(89) Fox. *Arch. Camb.* 1928, p. 145.

CHAPTER VII

Italy and Sardinia:

(90) Articles by TARAMELLI and BOSCH-GIMPERA in *Il Convegno Archeologico in Sardegna*, Reggio nell' Emilia, 1929.

(91) RANDALL-MACIVER. *Villanovans and Early Etruscans*. Oxford, 1924.

(92) Huelva. *Real.* s.v.

(93) Hoards. *B.P.* XLVII.

(94) Razor. *MA.* IX, p. 135.

(95) Nuraghi. TARAMELLI. In *M.A.* XIX.

(96) Hoards. —— In *M.A.* XXVII.

(97) Temple. —— In *M.A.* XXV.

Alpine Urnfields:

(98) WAGNER. "Prehistoric Fortifications in Bavaria." *Antiquity*, II, 5.

(99) STAMPFUSS. "Beiträge zur Nordgruppe der Urnenfelder-kultur." *Mannus Ergänzungsband*, v, Leipzig.

(100) ISCHER. *Die Pfahlbauten des Bielersees*. Biel, 1928.

(101) CHANTRE. *Études paléoethnologiques dans le bassin du Rhône, Age du bronze*. Lyons, 1875.

(102) Pouges les-Eaux. *Mat.* 1879, p. 386.

Scandinavia and North Germany:

(103) NORDEN. "Neue Ergebnisse der schwedischen Felsbildfor-schung," *IPEK*. 1927.

(104) SCHMIDT, H. "Die Luren von Daberkow." *PZ.* VII.

South Russia:

(105) TALLGREN. *La Pontide préscythique (Eurasia Septentrionalis Antiqua*, II). Helsingfors, 1926.

Siberia:

(106) MERHARDT, VON. *Die Bronzezeit am Jenessei*. Vienna, 1926.

Great Britain:

(107) CRAWFORD. "A Bronze Age Invasion." *Ant. J.* I.

(108) CRAWFORD AND KEILLER. *Wessex from the Air*. Oxford, 1927.

(109) PITT-RIVERS. *Excavations at Cranbourne Chase*. Vol. III.

(110) CLAY, R. C. C. "The Woodminton Group of Barrows." *WAM*, XLIII.

(111) CUNNINGTON. *All Cannings Cross*. Devizes, 1923.

(112) FOX. "An Encrusted Urn of the Bronze Age from Wales." *Ant. J.* VII.

(113) WOLSELEY. "Prehistoric...settlements on Park Brow." *Arch.* LXXVI.

INDEX